The
Crazy Eating
COOKBOOK

Crazy Cooking Essentials

Food

~ 100% grass fed meats

~ Pasture-raised pork, chicken, & duck
   and their fat

~ Eggs from pasture-raised chickens & ducks

~ Raw grass fed butter, cheese, kefir, & heavy cream

~ Organic 5% vegetables

~ Organic herbs & spices

~ Southern hemisphere fish if available

Tools

~ Knives, chef's & paring
~ Cutting boards, meat and general
~ Food scoop
~ Skillets, medium & large
~ Spatulas, metal & rubber
~ Saucepans, small & medium
~ Wooden spoon
~ Chinese soup spoon
~ Stockpot
~ Ladle
~ Instant pot, pressure cooker, slow cooker, or Dutch oven
~ Food processor
~ Blender with glass pitcher or immersion blender
~ Mortar and pestle/molcajete or garlic press
~ Japanese mandoline

ISBN: 978-1076 9138 07

Editor: Laila Weir, www.linkedin.com/in/laila-weir/

Book design: Jean Boles, jean.bolesbooks@gmail.com

Citations, index & bibliography format: Julie Webb, www.upwork.com/fl/juliewebb

Cover illustration: Miki Kingsley, mikinkingsley@gmail.com

Contents

Thank You!

- **To Alice Waters**

  whose Chez Panisse restaurant around the corner from my house, provided awesome pleasures of real food prepared with care, for over forty years.

- **To Kim Klaver**

  who gave me unflagging support and ongoing feedback of inestimable value. I could never have done it without you.

- **To Floreni Arevalo**

  my faithful kitchen ally—skilled slicer, chopper, dicer and fearless Instant Pot master!

- **To my nutrition book club associates** who contributed recipes for this cookbook

Tamar Cohen	Kris Homme
Laura Knoff	Edi Pfeiffer
Nori Hudson	Heather Holt

  and who, along with

  Srinika Narayan and Alla Marinow

  every six weeks over ten years, prepared scrumptious potluck dishes and carried on animated nutrition conversations that kept my food fire burning bright.

- **To my publishing team extraordinaire**

  Editor Laila Weir

  Book designer Jean Boles

  Indexer Julie Webb

  Book cover illustrator Miki Kingsley

  for exceptional work way beyond my expectations.

- **And to my clients and students**

  who trusted me enough to venture outside their comfort zone incorporating unfamiliar foods that promised better health, weight and energy.

For Kim

with a heart full of gratitude

The

Crazy Eating

COOKBOOK

Dr. Heidi Dulay

Nitty Gritty 1: 5% Vegetables[*]

These veggies have only five percent carbs—a boon to low-carbers.

Asparagus
Beet greens
Broccoli
Brussels sprouts
Cabbage
Cauliflower
Celery
Chard
Chicory
Cucumber
Dandelion
Eggplant
Endive
Escarole
Leeks
Lettuce
Mushroom
Mustard greens
Okra
Radishes
Rhubarb
Sorrel
Spinach
Sprouts
String beans
Summer squash
Tomatoes
Turnip greens
Watercress
Zucchini

[*] Mostly from Bernard Jensen (2000). *Guide to Diet and Detoxification.* New York: McGraw Hill.

Nitty Gritty 2: Percent of Net Carbs in Fruit

	Percent Net Carbs in Fruit				
1%					
2%					
3%					
4%					
5%	Raspberry	Blackberry			
6%	Strawberry	Coconut meat	Lemon		
7%	Cantaloupe	Watermelon			
8%	Peach				
9%	Orange				
10%	Cherries	Clementine	Plum		
11%					
12%	Blueberry	Pineapple	Apple	Pear	Kiwi
13%	Mango				
14%					
15%					
16%	Grapes				
17%					
18%					
19%					
20%	Banana				

References

Analida. "Moroccan Chicken Tagine Recipe." *Analida's Ethnic Spoon*, May 9, 2019. https://ethnicspoon.com/moroccan-chicken-tagine/.

Aobadia, Anne. "Keto Cheesecake with Blueberries." *Diet Doctor*, July 16, 2019. https://www.dietdoctor.com/recipes/low-carb-cheesecake/.

Benlafquih, Christine. "How to Cook in a Moroccan Tagine." *The Spruce Eats*, June 27, 2019. https://www.thespruceeats.com/cooking-in-a-moroccan-tagine-steps-2395002/.

Boerner, Leigh. "The Complicated Question of Drugs in the Water," Public Broadcasting System (PBS). May 14, 2014. https://www.pbs.org/wgbh/nova/article/pharmaceuticals-in-the-water/.

Boldt, Ethan. "What Are Nightshade Vegetables? How to Find Out If You're Sensitive to Them." *Dr. Axe Food & Medicine.* April 25, 2018. https://draxe.com/nutrition/vegetables/nightshade-vegetables/.

Chan, Laurie et al. *First Nations Food, Nutrition & Environmental Study: Results from Ontario 2011-2012.* Ottawa: University of Ottawa. 2014.

Child, Julia. *The Way to Cook.* New York: Knopf. 1989.

Clark, Melissa. "Tagine." *The New York Times.* nytimes.com. February 12, 2017. https://cooking.nytimes.com/recipes/1018513-lamb-tagine.

Diamond, Harvey and Marilyn. *Fit for Life.* Lebanon, IN: Grand Central Life and Style/Hachette. 1985.

Diamond, Marilyn and Donald Schnell. *Young for Life. The Easy, No-Diet, No-Sweat Plan to Look and Feel 10 Years Younger.* Emmaus, PA: Rodale. 2013.

Dulay, Heidi. *Crazy Eating in the Land of Foodlike Substances.* Marina del Rey, CA: Nada Productions. 2019.

Dulay, Heidi. *Crazy Eating. What Should I Eat? so I Never Have to Think about My Weight or Energy Again.* Marina del Rey, CA: Nada Productions. 2019.

Emmerich, Maria. *Keto Instant Pot: 130+ Healthy Low-Carb Recipes for your Electric Pressure Cooker or Slow Cooker.* Las Vegas, NV: Victory Belt. 2019.

Emmerich, Maria. *Keto Comfort Foods: Family Favorite Recipes Made Low Carb and Healthy.* Las Vegas, NV: Victory Belt. 2017

Emmerich, Maria. *Keto Restaurant Favorites: More than 175 Tasty Classic Recipes Made Fast, Fresh, and Healthy.* Las Vegas, NV: Victory Belt. 2017.

Ferro, Pamela and Raman Prasad. *The SCD for Autism and ADHD: A Reference and Dairy-Free Cookbook for the Specific Carbohydrate Diet.* Arlington, MA: Swallowtail. 2015.

Jensen, Bernard. *Guide to Diet and Detoxification.* New York: McGraw Hill. 2000.

Keller, Thomas. *Ad Hoc at Home. Family-Style Recipes.* New York: Artisan/Workman. 2009.

López-Alt, J. Kenji. *The Food Lab. Better Home Cooking Through Science.* New York: Norton. 2015.

Mattox, Charlyne. "Cauliflower Soup with Toasted Garlic." *Real Simple*, January 2013.

McGee, Harold. *On Food and Cooking. The Science and Lore of the Kitchen.* New York: Scribner. 2004.

McLagan, Jennifer. *Bitter. A Taste of the World's Most Dangerous Flavor, with Recipes.* Berkeley, CA: Ten Speed. 2014.

McLagan, Jennifer. *Fat. An Appreciation of a Misunderstood Ingredient.* Berkeley, CA: Ten Speed. 2008.

McLagan, Jennifer. *Bones. Recipes, History and Lore.* New York: Morrow/Harper Collins. 2005.

Mercola, Joseph. "Fluoride: Poison on Tap." mercola.com. October 14, 2017. https://articles.mercola.com/archive/2017/10/14/fluoride-poison-on-tap-documentary.aspx.

Mercola, Joseph. "How Your Microwave Oven Damages Your Health in Multiple Ways." mercola.com. May 18, 2010. https://articles.mercola.com/sites/articles/archive/2010/05/18/microwave-hazards.aspx

Mims, Ben. *Air Fry Every Day: 75 Recipes to Fry, Roast and Bake Using Your Air Fryer. A Cookbook.* New York: Clarkson Potter. 2018.

Morell, Sally Fallon and Kaayla Daniels. *Nourishing Broth: An Old-Fashioned Remedy for the Modern World.* New York: Grand Central Life & Style/Hachette. 2014.

Morell, Sally Fallon and Mary G. Enig. *Nourishing Traditions: The Cookbook that Challenges Politically Correct Nutrition and Diet Dictocrats.* New Trends Publishing: Washington, D.C. 2001.

Nosrat, Samin. *Salt Fat Acid Heat: Mastering the Elements of Good Cooking.* New York: Simon & Schuster. 2017.

Pescatore, Fred. "Buyer Beware: "BPA-Free Products Are Every Bit as Dangerous." *Logical Alternatives*, Volume 6, Issue 8, August 31. 2016.

Rosso, Julee and Sheila Lukins. *The Silver Palate Cookbook. Delicious Recipes, Menus, Tips, Lore from Manhattan's Celebrated Gourmet Food Shop.* New York: Workman. 1982.

Ruhlman, Michael. *Ruhlman's Twenty. 20 Techniques, 100 Recipes. A Cook's Manifesto.* San Francisco: Chronicle. 2011.

Russell, Sarah and Kristen Homme. "Mercury, the quintessential anti-nutrient." *Townsend Letter*, January 2017. www.townsendletter.com/Jan2017/mercury0117.html

Stafford, Gemma. "How to Make Cream Cheese (Bold Baking Basics)." *Gemma's Bigger Bolder Baking,* January 10, 2019. https://www.biggerbolderbaking.com/how-to-make-cream-cheese/.

Terry, Beth. *Plastic Free: How I Kicked the Plastic Habit and How You Can Too,* New York: Sky Horse. 2015.

Waters, Alice. *The Art of Simple Food. Notes, Lessons, and Recipes from a Delicious Revolution.* New York: Clarkson Potter. 2007.

Waters, Alice. *Chez Panisse Vegetables.* New York: Harper Collins. 1996.

Williams, Liz. *The One-Pot Ketogenic Diet Cookbook.* Berkeley, CA: Rockridge. 2018

Index

Also by Dr. Heidi Dulay

These books are a shining culmination of Dr. Heidi's years of education, research, sourcing, cooking, and savoring food that is healthy and life-giving.

Dr. Heidi earned a doctorate in human development education from Harvard University, a master's in management from Stanford, and top nutrition consultant certification from Bauman College.

A veteran university professor, retreat director, journal article writer, and clinical nutritionist, Dr. Heidi now spends her time writing and helping a few private clients and groups improve their lives through eating.

Does her *Crazy Eating* teachings work? … People say she and her same-age partner look at least twenty years younger than their 74 years. They wear the same size clothes as in college, take no medication at all, are full of energy, and continue to grow their own businesses. Success stories of her clients and students abound.

drheidi@thecrazyeatingbook.com

Introduction

I f you've been eating healthy and still can't fit into your favorite pants, read on. I have good news! It turns out that many foods on our Avoid lists are actually fat burners and energy boosters. And many "healthy" foods that we feel we must eat make us fat, foggy and slow. For decades, we've had it wrong coming and going. I present these ideas in the first two Crazy Eating books with hundreds of examples and much scientific support.

Now it's time to apply those ideas in the kitchen!

This cookbook is brimming with recipes that include butter and lard, red meat, eggs, chocolate, coffee, and salt! You won't see rice (including brown), bread (even whole grain), or yogurt. And only the lowest-carb fruits make the grade.

Crazy Eaters don't do "plates" or "pyramids." Instead we enjoy fatty meats, full fat dairy, and as many eggs as we want. In fact, most of the appetite suppressants in this cookbook are "fat bombs." Because *qualified* fats are a must for health and brainpower. "Lean protein" is lean only compared to protein that is **_abnormally_** fatty from the effects of grain feed on animal fat. Lean protein really is healthy-fat protein!

Sugar is nowhere in this book. It is totally unnecessary in main dishes, sides, or spreads. Even in desserts, its absence is hardly noticeable. Fat takes its place! With fat, food is delicious and cooking becomes exciting again.

We're generous with salt because it is a mineral powerhouse and gives smooth energy. Qualified salt is good for the heart and the adrenals.

What's "qualified"? It's food that's clean and real, keeps its natural fats, and contains nutrients in their natural proportions. It's food our ancestors preferred.

I am not a chef. I have cooked in restaurant kitchens only as a student taking cooking classes—a week in the vegan kitchen of the Green Gulch Zen Center in Mill Valley, a couple of weeks with a teaching chef in a small restaurant in upstate New York, and a 12-class basic series taught by Chef Olivier Said, owner of the Berkeley cooking school Kitchen on Fire. All the classes were fun and informative, but in the end, it has been the daily practice of cooking home meals that forms the foundation of the *Crazy Eating Cookbook.*

I enjoy the instant gratification and the creativity of cooking, but mostly I cook in self-defense—against a world filled with foodlike substances. I want to live much longer than my 74 years, and I want my loved ones around! I can't leave it to commercial establishments who keep their eye on their bottom line. So, most every day, I happily cook the food my family eats.

I hope this book inspires you in your kitchen. ...

Shall we cook?

Important note: Before you use any recipe, remember:

1. **The ingredients should always be "qualified."**
   - **Eggs, poultry and pork**: pasture-raised, i.e., pigs, chickens and other poultry are on pasture all day.
   - **Meat** (beef, lamb, buffalo, bison, venison): 100% grass-fed or wild.
   - **Olive oil**: either extra virgin or virgin, and organically grown.
   - **Lard (pork fat), schmaltz (chicken fat) or other animal fat**: from 100% grass-fed or pastured animals.
   - **Ghee and butter**: grass-fed. If not used for cooking, butter should also be raw.
   - **Dairy (milk, cream, cheese, kefir**): grass-fed and raw, unless used for cooking.
   - **Vegetables, herbs and fruits**: organically grown.
   - **Salt**: either Himalayan (pink) or RealSalt from Redmond, Utah.[1]
   - **Black pepper**: freshly ground peppercorns.
   - **Monk fruit extract** refers to Lo Han Supreme by NuNaturals, the purest I've found.
   - **Water**: filtered, preferably through reverse osmosis with remineralization, natural spring water, or sparkling water with no additives; in *glass* bottles.[2]
   - **Garlic and onion** are prepared—peeled, sliced, chopped or minced— about 10 minutes before cooking—to release the biologically active ingredient[3] in them that promotes heart health and blood sugar balance.
   - **Scallions**: include the roots with the stalk. They contain a lot of nutrients.

2. **Ingredients** appear in the recipes *as they are used,* not in a list at the beginning. They are bolded to make it easy for you to see them as you scan the recipe. Alice Waters uses this system and I have found it most efficient when I cook. It eliminates duplication of information and having to go from the procedures back to a list for quantities.

3. **Tools** also appear as they are used in the recipe, bolded and italicized. When the tool is not mentioned, the activity is bolded and italicized, e.g., "*peel*" implies a vegetable peeler.

---

[1] I do not recommend Celtic (gray) salt because it is harvested from ocean water, which, especially in the Northern Hemisphere, may be polluted.
[2] Do NOT drink water in plastic bottles. We don't know how long the water has been in the bottle—in the warehouse or on the store shelf—at risk for contamination from plasticizers gradually leaching into the water.
[3] Allicin

4. ***"Mise en place"*** is the first step in every Crazy Eating recipe. This French phrase is a standard teaching in culinary school. It means "to put in place"—gather and arrange the ingredients and tools needed for cooking, to maximize efficiency. Professional chefs, for whom every minute counts, always start their work with *mise en place.*[4]

One last thing, if you don't have a food scoop, two cutting boards, and chef's knife, you might want to invest in them before you start. They'll be your faithful kitchen workhorses.

MAIN DISH SMORGASBORD

Eggs, Meat, Chicken, Fish, or Pizza?

What's for dinner?

What's for breakfast?

Pancakes, Eggs, and Pizza

An eater's best friend …

egg

**Crazy Eating delivers eggs in many forms,
from guilt-free pancakes
to crustless quiche.**

Skinny Pancakes

Eat pancakes and not add an inch or pound? Well, there *is* a way… Skinny pancakes don't taste fake; they're delightfully savory, but feel like pancakes. They take all the guilt away and leave all the pleasure.

This recipe is adapted from "Zucchini Pancakes" in the *Practical Paleo* cookbook by Diane Sanfilippo. You can also make them with asparagus, mushroom, or spinach. Eat them straight up, or with a big dollop of sour cream, or with tomato sauce if you can eat nightshades.

SERVES 4

When to start: 25 minutes before enjoying
Hands-on time: 15 minutes
Stove time: 5 minutes

PREP

Mise en place.

Start warming serving plates.

Optional:
Prepare a sauce:
   ◆ Warm up tomato sauce or other sauce
     OR
     Take your homemade Pure Sour Cream (see recipe) out of the fridge.

Using a ***food processor or grater***, shred
   ◆ **2 medium Zucchini—to yield 1¾ cups shredded**

Heat ***large pan*** on medium low (325° F) and add
   ◆ **2 Tb Ghee or taste-free coconut oil**

In ***medium bowl***, add and mix together with ***wire whisk*** (***fork*** takes a lot longer)
   ◆ **3 Eggs**

- **1 Tb + 1 tsp Coconut flour or green banana flour**
- **To taste salt and pepper**
- Mix in well the shredded zucchini

COOK

Ladle batter into heated pan to make 1 big pancake, or 4 individual pancakes.

Use *spatula* to distribute the zucchini evenly across the pancake(s). Set *timer* for 2 minutes.

Shake pan so pancake(s) slide and don't stick. Check bottom of pancakes for golden brown.

If you know how, flip the big pancake over; otherwise, cut it into 4 by making a cross with the spatula. Flip each piece or the 4 small pancakes. Set timer for one minute.

Check for doneness and slide the finished pancakes onto the heated plates.

SERVE

Serve plain or with a sauce and other accompaniments like sausage, bacon, arugula...

Enjoy!

Self-Basted Eggs

This is how I usually cook eggs. Unlike frying, basting eggs cooks the yolk without having to flip the egg, leaving it undamaged and looking beautiful. It also creates a lovely pink film over the yolk, softening the raw look of sunny-side up. And it's less work...

SERVES 2

When to start: 8 minutes before enjoying
Hands-on time: 4 minutes
Stove time: 4 minutes

PREP

Mise en place.

Optional:
If you are cooking for a finicky person, crack the eggs into a *bowl* and remove the little white snot-like muscles that you see on the yolks, usually on the sides, taking great care not to break the yolk. (They're protein but look nasty.)

Start warming the serving plates.

Start preparing any accompaniments so that they're ready when the eggs are done.

COOK

Heat on medium a *skillet that has a cover* that fits the number of eggs you want to cook.

Add

- **1-2 Tb Ghee, bacon fat, or lard** to cover the bottom of the pan
- **4 eggs**
- **1 Tb Liquid: water or broth**

Cover the pan, turn the heat down low, and set a *timer* to 4 minutes. Don't open the pan until the timer rings.

When the timer rings, turn off the heat, and check the eggs for doneness. If necessary, leave them in the skillet a bit longer, where they will continue to cook off the heat.

SERVE

Transfer the eggs to individual serving plates. Arrange the accompaniments (if any) around the eggs.

Enjoy!

Zucchini-Bottom Eggs

A quick and pretty breakfast, or lunch or dinner …Sliced zucchini is the quickest vegetable to prepare. You simply wash it. No peeling. With a simple mandoline (see in the Tools section), you can slice it in half a minute, and cook it in just a few more minutes. It's a soft complement to the bold taste of eggs.

zucchini

SERVES 2

When to start: 12 minutes before enjoying
Hands-on time: 6 minutes
Stove time: 6 minutes

PREP

Mise en place.

Wash and slice with a **mandoline** or **knife**
  ◆ **1 large or 2 medium Zucchini**

Crack into a **bowl**
  ◆ **4 Eggs**

If you like, remove the muscle holding the yolk to the white.

Start warming the serving plates.

COOK

Heat on medium a *large skillet* (to fit the zucchini spread out on the bottom).

Turn the heat down to medium low and add
- **2 Tb Cooking fat** (lard, ghee or coconut oil)
- The sliced zucchini, spreading the slices to cover the bottom of the pan

Season the zucchini generously with
- **Salt, other powdered herbs and spices you like**[5]

Crack (or slide) on top of the zucchini the prepped eggs

Cover and cook 3-5 minutes or until the egg yolks are almost the firmness you like. Don't open the pan during this time.

SERVE

When almost done, immediately transfer the zucchini-bottom eggs to the warmed serving plates. They will continue to cook a bit more.

Enjoy!

---

[5] I use my ready mix of garlic, onion, fennel, rosemary and thyme powders.

Scramble Soirée (Omelet-Frittata-Quiche)

All are variations on the theme of sautéed veggies in scrambled eggs enriched with heavy cream. An *omelet* is the quickest, but requires some manual dexterity and practice to do well. Since *quiche* became crustless, it has grown indistinguishable from a *frittata*. Neither requires much skill, just a bit more time for the oven to do the cooking. You could also forego looks and just pour beaten eggs and cream into a pan with sautéed veggies and have a fine *scramble* in a few minutes.

The first steps apply to all the variations.

SERVES 2

Start the recipe: 20 minutes before enjoying
Hands-on time: 10 minutes
Stove time: 13 minutes

PREP

Mise en place.

Warm your serving plates.

Wash and **slice** or **chop**
  ◆ **1 cup Veggies:** onion, asparagus, spinach, mushroom, bell pepper etc.

COOK

Heat a **9" skillet** and add
  ◆ **2 Tb Ghee, lard, schmaltz, bacon fat or olive oil**

Start sautéing the prepped veggies.

While the veggies are cooking, in a **bowl**, crack and slightly beat
  ◆ **4 Eggs**

Add
  ◆ **1 Tb Heavy cream**
  ◆ **To taste Salt and pepper**

Optional: Grate
  ◆ **¼ cup cheese:** sharp cheddar, goat, parmesan or your choice

Omelet

When veggies are cooked (about 10 minutes), push them to one side of the pan with your spatula and add the beaten eggs.

COOK

Swirl the pan so the egg spreads over the bottom; lift the edges and tilt the pan so the uncooked egg rolls to the bottom and gets cooked.

When the egg is almost done (still moist), spoon the veggies onto the egg, sprinkle the grated cheese over them (optional), and fold the egg over the veggies (and cheese).

SERVE

Slide the omelet onto a serving plate, divide and place half onto a second serving plate.

Serve with a fresh green salad or a warm side dish. (Select from Sides ...)

Can top the omelet with salsa, pesto, tomato or other sauce.

Enjoy!

Frittata

PREP

Pre-heat oven to 350° F.

Grease a **pie pan** with fat of your choice. Follow the steps above that apply to all the variations.

When veggies are cooked, cool them a couple of minutes, transfer them to the pie pan and pour the egg mixture over the veggies.

Stir to distribute evenly.

Optional:
Sprinkle with grated cheese.

COOK

Bake 20-25 minutes until the eggs look puffy and jiggle a bit in the middle when you shake the pan.

SERVE

Transfer frittata to a warm serving plate, garnish with herbs (e.g., parsley, basil) and cut into serving pieces.

Serve plain, or with salsa, pesto, sour cream or other sauce.

Serve with a fresh green salad or a warm side dish. (Select from Sides …)

Enjoy!

Crustless Quiche

Without the crust, a quiche is almost identical to a frittata. The differences are: 1) quiche recipes (except the one here) use milk instead of cream (even though cream works as well, if not better) 2) frittata recipes add the egg mixture to the veggies, while quiche recipes add the veggies to the egg mixture, and 3) for quiche, cheese is added to the egg mixture from the start, while frittata recipes do so just before baking. Here's how to make crustless quiche.

PREP

Follow the steps above that apply to all the variations.

Optional:
Add the cheese to the beaten eggs and mix well.

Stir in the sautéed veggies.

Pour the mixture into a **9" greased pie plate** or **quiche dish**.

COOK

Bake at 350˚ 40-45 minutes or until a knife inserted in the center comes out clean.

SERVE

Cut into serving wedges.

Serve with a fresh green salad or a warm side dish. (See Sides.)

Enjoy!

Yes, Pizza!

It's the crust—not the cheese—that makes pizza fattening. Wheat flour (containing gluten) or some other non-glutinous grain flour is its traditional main ingredient. Instead, Yes, Pizza!'s crust uses eggs and cheese, plus optional grated cauliflower.

A pizza has four layers: 1) the crust, 2) the underlying sauce, 3) cheese, and 4) the topping. The traditional underlying sauce is tomato paste or tomato sauce, but pesto is becoming a trendy alternate. The cheese is often mozzarella. Traditional toppings are sausage (pepperoni pizza) or tomato slices (pizza margherita) with olives, onions, or herbs. Be as creative as you like! Just stay away from potato or pineapple topping ... use meat, avocado, or other keto-paleo ingredients you like.

SERVES 6

When to start: 40 minutes before enjoying
Hands-on time: 10 minutes
Stove time: 30 minutes

PREP

Preheat oven to 350° F.

Mise en place.

Line **a baking sheet** or **11-inch pizza pan** with **parchment paper**.

THE CRUST

In a **small bowl**, lightly beat
  ♦ **2-3 Eggs**

Optional:
In **food processor** grate and put in **large bowl**
  ♦ **½ Cauliflower (4¾ oz. yield)**

Grate
  ♦ **5¼-6 oz Cheese: mozzarella, cheddar or your choice**

If using cauliflower for the crust, use the *smaller* amount of eggs and cheese.

Add to bowl and stir well:
- **2/3 of the grated cheese**
- The beaten eggs
- The grated cauliflower if using
- **½ tsp salt**

Using a *spatula,* spread mixture thinly on the baking sheet/pizza pan.

COOK

Bake 20 mins or until lightly browned.

THE FILLING

Slice and set aside
- **1 White onion**
- **1 Green or yellow bell pepper**
- **Handful Black olives**[6]
- **2 Tb Fresh basil or arugula** (OR 1 Tb dried
- **oregano**)

Spread over the crust to about half an inch
of the edge
- **2-3 Tb No-Tomato sauce** (see recipe), **tomato sauce**
- **or tomato paste**

OR
- **2-3 Tb Poly Pesto** (see recipe)

black olives

Top with the rest of the shredded cheese and the sliced onions, bell pepper, and olives.
Increase oven temp to 420º F and bake pizza 5-10 mins or until cheese is melted.

Garnish generously with **1 Tb Fresh basil or arugula** (or 1 Tb dried oregano).

Enjoy!

---

[6] Organic pitted Peruvian Botija black olives are my favorite.

Meat

Uncelebrated richest source of nutrients

Good Ole Meat Loaf

I love meat loaf. It's simple to cook, easy to eat, and inexpensive. It also provides meals for several days. I can even simulate a cheeseburger (no bun, of course) by melting cheese on a slice of meatloaf.

SERVES 8

When to start: 90 minutes before enjoying
Hands-on time: 15 minutes
Stove time: 60 minutes

PREP

Mise en place.

Preheat oven to 375º F.

ground beef

Chop
   ◆ **2 Yellow onions**
   ◆ **2 Zucchini**

In a ***large bowl***, mix together
just until ingredients are combined
(overmixing makes the meat loaf tough)
   ◆ **2 lbs. Ground beef or any meat**
   ◆ **2 Eggs**
   ◆ The chopped onions and zucchini

Optional:
   ◆ **½ pound Ground liver** (This is a good way to sneak liver into your family's diet!)

Season the mixture with
   ◆ **1 Tb   Onion powder**
   ◆ **1 Tb   Garlic powder**
   ◆ **2 Tb   Coconut aminos**
   ◆ **To taste Any other herbs or spices you like, e.g. thyme**

Transfer mixture to a ***9" x 5" loaf pan*** to mold the loaf.

Line a **baking sheet** with **parchment paper**, place it over the loaf and invert the pan so the loaf falls onto the baking sheet.[7]

COOK

Bake the meat loaf for about 1 hour or until it reaches 160° F.

While the meat loaf is cooking, heat
- **1 jar Tomato sauce[8] of your choice**

Or
- **1 jar Tomato paste and**
- **To taste: Coconut aminos, salt, pepper, and (optional) hot sauce**

Optional:
Mince for garnish
- **2 Tb Parsley leaves**

Put the meat loaf on a **cutting board** and let rest 10-15 minutes.

SERVE

Slice the meat loaf.

Place one or two slices on each plate, top with the tomato sauce, and garnish with parsley.

Enjoy!

---

[7] We don't bake the meat in the loaf pan because it would steam instead of bake.

[8] Tomato can leach toxic substances in can linings, therefore, we recommend using tomato products packed in glass jars. Amazon carries a selection.

Crazy Cheeseburger

(Based on the recipe for Classic Keto Hamburger from dietdoctor.com.)

Crazy cheeseburgers are a health food. But commercial cheeseburgers are most often not—they're usually made with feedlot beef and cheese whose fat composition is unnatural and harmful, all riddled with pesticides. The bun is no better, made with refined conventional wheat.

A Crazy cheeseburger is made from 100% grass-fed cheese and beef (or lamb, buffalo or bison) free of pesticides, whose fat composition mirrors nature. It contains spices, minced herbs and veggies mixed in with the meat, and is served on keto almond flour buns or lettuce leaves.

Makes 8 four-ounce cheeseburgers (freeze extras)

THE BUNS
When to start: 90 minutes before enjoying
Hands-on time: 15 minutes
Stove time: 60 minutes

PREP
Preheat the oven to 350° F.

Mise en place.

Prepare a **baking sheet (or two)** to fit the buns when they're done and set aside.

Bring to a boil
  - **1¼ cups Filtered water**

Separate the whites (store the yolks to use for other recipes[9]) from
  - **3 Eggs**

In a **medium bowl**, mix together
  - **1¼ cups Almond flour**
  - **5 Tb Psyllium husk powder**
  - **2 tsp Baking powder**
  - **1 tsp Salt**

---

[9] E.g., Cozy Custard, Cheesecake

Add while beating with a ***hand mixer*** for about 30 seconds, to Play-Doh consistency
- **The boiling water**
- **2 tsp White wine vinegar or cider vinegar**
- **3 Egg whites**

Don't overmix.

Moisten your hands and separate the dough into 8 pieces. Form each piece into the shape of a bun and place on the baking sheet, leaving room for the buns to double in size.

sesame seeds

Optional: Sprinkle on top
- **1 Tb Sesame seeds**

COOK

Bake on lower rack 50-60 minutes. Tap the bottom of a bun for a hollow sound that tells you they're done.

Let them cool, then cut in half.

THE BURGERS
When to start: 45 minutes before enjoying
Hands-on time: 30 minutes
Stove time: 15 minutes

PREP
Mise en place.

Mince
- **1 large Onion**
- **1 head (10 cloves) Garlic**
- **2 cups Zucchini** (2 cups minced)
- **1 cup Cabbage or other leafy vegetable**

Optional:
Separate the leaves and wash
- **1 head Butter lettuce or other lettuce for garnish**

Slice
- **12-16 ounces Cheese** (cheddar or your preference)
- **1-2 Red onions for garnish**

- ◆ **1-2 Tomatoes for garnish**
- ◆ Tip: Use a ***mandoline*** to control thickness.

In a ***large bowl***, add and mix together, preferably with your hands
- ◆ **2 lbs Ground beef, lamb, bison, or buffalo**
- ◆ **The prepped veggies**
- ◆ **2 tsp Himalayan salt or RealSalt**
- ◆ **2 Tbsp Any spices you like** (readymixes[10] are great)

Mix until just combined. Overmixing may toughen the meat.

Divide the mixture into 8 equal chunks.

Pat each chunk into ¾-1" thick patties. Press the middle of each one to create an indentation—to prevent forming a ball-shaped burger.

COOK

Heat a ***skillet*** on medium high and add
- ◆ **1 Tb Fat: ghee, lard or coconut oil**

Slide patties into the skillet, leaving space around each patty to prevent steaming. The meat should sizzle as it hits the pan.

Cook until brown on the bottom, about 3-5+ minutes depending on your choice of rare, medium rare, medium, or well done.

With a ***metal spatula***, flip the patties and add the cheese slices, cooking an additional 3-5+ minutes. If the cheese is not melting enough, cover the pan during the last minute or two.

SERVE

Serve cheeseburger as-is or with Mayo Verde, tomato, and onion, accompanied by a cucumber salad. (See cucumber salad recipes in Sides.)

Enjoy!

---

[10] A readymix is a mix of spices you prepare in advance and store in your pantry. For example, the simplest is garlic and onion powder. I also keep a mix of garlic, onion, fennel, rosemary, sage, thyme, and turmeric, as well as Moroccan spice mix of cinnamon, nutmeg, coriander, turmeric, and saffron.

Maria's Minchi

Minchi is a dish of loose ground meat[11] and chopped vegetables, my sister's eternal favorite. It is a prized dish in Macau, an autonomous territory of China[12] that comprises the most populated area in the world.[13] My maternal grandpa was born and raised in Macau. When he moved to the Philippines to find his fortune, he brought with him his love for minchi.

I've tweaked our family recipe just a bit here ...

SERVES 6-8 (freeze in meal-size portions what you won't consume in 3 or 4 days)

When to start: 30 minutes before enjoying
Hands-on time: 15 minutes
Stove time: 15 minutes

PREP

Mise en place.

Chop to match approximately the size of the ground meat pieces
- **4 cloves Garlic**
- **1 medium Onion,** any color, including green
- **2 large Carrots**
- **2 large Zucchini or summer squash**
- **2 large Bay leaves,** fresh or dried

garlic

Optional:
- **2 Jalapeños or bell peppers**
- **Vegetable(s) you want to use up, e.g. cabbage**

COOK

In a ***large frying or sauté pan***, 2.5" high, heat on medium
- **1 Tb Ghee, coconut oil, beef fat, or lard**

When the oil shimmers or sizzles with a drop of water, add
- the prepped garlic, onions, carrot, jalapeño, and bay leaves.

---

[11] Usually beef or pork or a combination of both.
[12] Portugal turned rule over Macau over to China in 1999.
[13] Macau is part of Guangdong province in China, the core part of the Pearl River Delta, which includes Hong Kong, Guangzhou, Shenzhen and other major cities.

Cook about 5 minutes, stirring occasionally, until the onion is transparent and bay leaves slightly browned.

Mix in
- **2 lbs. Ground beef or pork, or 1 lb each**

Sprinkle on the meat
- **2 Tb Salt**
- **To taste Black pepper, freshly ground**
- **2 tsp Garlic powder**
- **2 tsp Onion powder**
- **3 tsp/1 Tb Cumin seed powder**
- **½ cup Coconut aminos**
- **¼ cup Red wine or red wine vinegar**

Optional:
- **¼ cup Tamarind concentrate/paste**[14]

Mix thoroughly, then add
- the zucchini and other veggies you prepped, and toss.

Cook a few minutes, then taste and adjust.

SERVE

Serve over Beats Rice or with Could Be Mashed Potato.

Enjoy!

"rice"

---

[14] Neera's, Rani's and Sambar brands come in glass jars

Fast Meat

Steak gives a giant return on kitchen time investment. The tender cuts—rib eye, rib, tenderloin, porterhouse and filet mignon—are prepared in minutes. The tougher cuts should be marinated at least two hours or overnight to tenderize them; nevertheless, tougher cuts like tender ones require little hands-on time and deliver wonderful flavor and big nutrition.[15]

Serves 4

When to start: If not marinating, 15-20 minutes before enjoying

                  If marinating, at least 2 hours and 15-20 minutes before enjoying

Hands-on time: 5-10 minutes

Stove time: 8-12 minutes

PREP

Mise en place.

If you're using a tougher cut, like hanger, flank, sirloin, or minute steak, or if you want maximum flavor for a tender cut like rib eye, entrecote, or tenderloin, marinate it first:

Mix in a ***glass bowl***
- ¼ **cup Coconut aminos**
- ¼ **cup Lemon juice or balsamic vinegar**
- ¼ **cup Olive oil**
- **2 tsp Garlic powder or 1 Tb minced fresh garlic**
- **1 tsp Salt**
- **½ tsp Black pepper, ground**

Add and soak in the marinade
- **4 4-5 oz. beef steaks**

Let soak at least 2 hours. If longer, refrigerate. It's ok to marinate up to a day or two. Then proceed …

If not marinating, skip the above and follow the directions below.

Put ***dinner plates*** in a warming oven.

----

[15] Almost all the nutrients required by our bodies can be found in meat.

Optional:

Mince and set aside (if not marinating the meat)
- ◆ **1 clove Garlic**
- ◆ **1 Tb Rosemary**

Season both sides of the meat generously with
- ◆ Salt and pepper

Optional:
- ◆ Daily Readymix or L'il Readymix (see recipes in **Accents and Sauces** section) or any other herbs and spices you like

COOK
- -
Heat a ***medium skillet*** over medium high heat, add the steak and cook about 4 mins, until it is nicely browned.

Flip and, if not marinated, sprinkle on the steak
- ◆ The minced garlic and rosemary

Baste
- ◆ with the juice and cook another minute.

Cover the pan, lower the heat, and cook about 3 minutes more for medium rare.

Transfer the steak to the serving plates and let rest in the warming oven about 5 minutes.

Deglaze the pan with water, broth, or wine.

SERVE
- -
If the steaks are thick, you can slice them—your preference.

Spoon the juice over the meat.

Add green salad and/or other veggie accompaniments and serve.

Enjoy!

Slow Meat

We're talking about any big chunk of meat—with or without bones. My vote is for bones—they deepen the flavor of the meat, and noshing away at the bone is so fun … Either way, slow cooking is a convenient way to cook cuts of meat that are not naturally tender, such as brisket, ribs, legs, shanks, chuck. It tenderizes meat so that it falls off the bone … Slow meat cooking takes a lot of stove time—but just a little of your time.

A **crockpot** has been the classic appliance for slow cooking. It simmers food on the countertop at a lower temperature than baking, boiling or frying, and can go unattended for many hours—even overnight. It turns itself off and keeps the food warm for hours. And it can be put away easily when not in use.

A **Wonderbag** functions like a crockpot without electricity—

beef shank

its unique insulated technology keeps food simmering up to 12 hours. Plus, made with native African material, it is beautiful and portable—I've taken it to potlucks (with food still simmering), where it easily became the center of attention. It was created to save poor families in South Africa the time they spend gathering firewood for cooking. Now available on Amazon, Wonderbag sales benefit a foundation that helps these families.

The newest kid on the slow cooking block is the **Instant Pot,** whose wide appeal is its compactness and versatility. You can steam vegetables, make yogurt, cook a roast, boil eggs, and even make a cake, all with only one appliance. And it allows you to brown meat before slow cooking, without having to use another pan—just press a different button.

Here's how to make it happen, no matter which appliance you use, including a big old pot on the stove.

SERVES 10-16

When to start: 1-8½ hours before enjoying
Hands-on time: 20-35 minutes
Stove time: 40 minutes - 8 hours

PREP

Note: Salting the meat 24 hours before cooking may give you juicier, more tender, more succulent results, and may shorten slow-cooking time an hour or more.[16]

Mise en place.

Peel, chop, and set aside
- ◆ **1 large Onion, any color, or 2 large leeks**
- ◆ **2 heads Garlic**
- ◆ **4 large Carrots,** cut into 2-inch pieces

Season
- ◆ **4 lbs. Meat** with
- ◆ **2 Tb Salt**
- ◆ **2 handfuls any herbs you like**

OR
- ◆ **2 Tb any powdered seasonings**

carrot

COOK

Optional: Brown the meat, about 15 minutes. Browning can be done in the same pot for all the appliances except the slow cooker, which has a clay bottom.

Add to the pot
- ◆ The prepped Garlic and onion
- ◆ The seasoned Meat—place on top of the garlic and onion
- ◆ The prepped Carrots—place around the meat
- ◆ **1-2 quarts Bone broth (beef, chicken or other; use the**
- ◆ **larger quantity for soup)**
- ◆ **½ cup Coconut aminos**
- ◆ **3 Bay leaves** (Tip: crease the leaves to release more flavor)

Optional:
- ◆ **2 cups Wine**

Cook the meat and veggies:

Slow cooker. Turn on low for 8 hours.

bay leaves

---

[16] See Samin Nosrat, *Salt Fat Acid Heat*, and Harold McGee, *On Food and Cooking.*

Wonderbag: Bring to a boil in a regular pot and high-simmer about 15 minutes. Then transfer pot to Wonderbag and close it up.

Instant Pot: Turn on low for 8 hours.

Big pot: Bring to a boil, then lower heat to a bare simmer for at least 3 hours or until done.

If using a **slow cooker**, start testing for doneness after 7 hours. The meat is done if it is tender or falling off the bone. If using a regular pot, start testing after 3 hours.
Taste juice and adjust seasonings if necessary.

SERVE

When done, put the meat on *a cutting board*, let rest about 15 minutes, then slice. (Resting allows the juices to spread evenly throughout the meat.)

Serve with the carrots and onion.

Enjoy!

Pork Belly Roast

Pork belly is a boneless, high-fat cut from the underside of the pig (not its stomach). It is a delicacy in many parts of the world, including China, Korea, and the Philippines. Did you know that bacon is sliced pork belly? Cured with salt and sometimes smoked and, unfortunately, often sweetened with maple syrup or another form of sugar.

Here, we simply roast the meat and use herbs and spices to enhance the naturally wonderful flavor of fat. You don't have to use your big oven. A four-pound roast fits in a countertop oven, air fryer, Instant Pot, Wonderbag, or slow cooker.

I made a pork belly roast when it was my turn to host a nutrition book club meeting. I had selected ketogenic diets ("keto" for short) as our discussion topic. What better to serve than a roast that naturally fulfilled the keto fat percentage requirement—70-80% fat? All eight nutritionists present asked for the recipe (below). One confided later that it had become her husband's favorite dish. Here's what she said:

"I would buy a large slab and put it in the slow cooker at night over low. In the morning, it was all a glorious gooey treat. I never browned before or after because it was soooo delicious. It didn't even need salt and pepper, which would have been good too. You need to put a warning on your recipe: one might eat the whole thing!"
– Nancy C, Oakland, California

You can just do what Nancy did and skip this recipe! Or:

SERVES 10-14

When to start:	one day before enjoying
Hands-on time:	30 minutes
Stove time:	3-8 hours, depending on cooking method

PREP

The day before cooking, or at least 4 hours before:

Mise en place.

Rinse and pat dry
- **4 pounds Pork belly**

Optional:

Score the rind: With a ***sharp knife***, make long, shallow, diagonal cuts across the rind, no more than 1/8 inch deep and ½ to 1 inch apart. Then make cuts across the cuts to form a grid. Scoring helps the seasonings and fat penetrate the meat while cooking.

Season the meat: Mix together, then rub all over the pork (ok to omit any seasonings).
- **2 ½ Tb Rosemary powder**
- **2 ½ Tb Thyme powder**
- **2 ½ Tb Sage powder**
- **2 Tb Fennel powder**
- **2 Tb Garlic powder**
- **1 Tb Onion powder**
- **2 Tb Himalayan salt or RealSalt**
- **1 Tb Black pepper**
- **2 Tb Olive oil, virgin**
- **3 Tb White wine or lemon juice**

Put the seasoned pork in a ***glass or ceramic container*** and put in fridge at least 4 hours; overnight is good.

COOK

Mise en place.

Select appliance: Oven or slow cooker. If ***oven,*** pre-heat to 450° F.

Peel and de-germ
- **2 heads Garlic**

Trim and *slice*
- **2 large Onions, any color**
- **1 bulb Fennel**
- **Fennel leaves—remove from main stalks**
- **3 stalks Celery**

Put in ***oven pan*** or ***slow cooker*** the prepped garlic, onions, fennel, fennel leaves, celery.

Dry the rind with paper towel.

Put the pork on top of the herbs.

OPTION 1 – OVEN

Roast 10 mins at 450° F or until the pork skin starts to bubble and turn golden brown. Then, lower temp to 325° F and roast for 1½ hours.

Optional:
Carefully open oven door and add into the tray
  ◆ **¾ cup White wine or ¼ cup lemon juice**

Continue cooking 1 hour.

Test to see if meat pulls apart easily. If not, continue roasting.

Optional:
To crisp skin, raise heat to 450° F about 15 mins, or broil. Watch it!

OPTION 2 – SLOW COOKER

Put meat into *slow cooker* and if you like, add ¾ cup white wine

Turn on Low 7 to 9 hours or overnight.

Test to see if the meat pulls apart easily. If not, continue cooking.

Optional: To crisp skin, preheat oven to broil and transfer roast to oven for about 10 mins—watch it!

SERVE

Transfer to a *wooden board* or *other non-plastic surface* to rest 15 minutes, to allow the juices in the roast to even out through the meat.

Can remove the crackling[17] and slice or break it up into pieces and serve separately. Slice pork belly and serve. Yummmmm. A big green salad goes well with it.

Enjoy!

---

[17] Crackling is the fatty skin on the top of a pork belly roast that turns golden brown and crispy when the roast is done. Crackling is commercially processed to produce pork rinds. The pork rinds sold by U.S. Wellness Meats are from pastured pork belly and are delicious.

DIY Bacon

Not too long ago, I went through all the packages of bacon in my supermarket[18] and couldn't believe that the bacon in ALL the packages contained some form of sugar—white, brown, turbinado, agave, or honey powder. Most were smoked. (Sadly, smoking can infuse food with carcinogenic substances.)

To include bacon in this health-focused cookbook, I decided to cure it myself ... I found a source of sugar-free, unsmoked, pasture-raised, sliced pork belly, and cured it with salt and lemon. Voila! DIY bacon. And it passed a taste test with my most finicky client.

MAKES 1 lb. – 9 slices 8¼" long, 1¼" wide, ¼" thick

When to start: 1 day (24.5 hours) before enjoying
Hands-on time: 20 minutes
Stove time: 10 minutes

PREP

<u>The day before cooking:</u>

Mise en place.

Into a **quart mason jar**, freshly **squeeze** the juice of
- **3 Lemons**

Spread out on a **baking pan** or on **wax paper** on your counter
- **1 pound Sliced fresh side pork bacon**[19] (available from U.S. Wellness Meats online)

Optional:
With **kitchen scissors**, cut the slices in half—for easier handling.

Sprinkle over and rub into the bacon
- **2 tsp Salt**

Stuff the bacon into the mason jar with the lemon juice, cover the jar and turn it over several times to wet the bacon slices thoroughly with the juice.

Refrigerate 24 hours,[20] turning the jar occasionally for a more even soak.

---

[18] Safeway Community Market, Shattuck Avenue, Berkeley, California
[19] Source: U.S. Wellness Meats, grasslandbeef.com: Sliced Fresh Side Pork Bacon (DIY Bacon). It contains one ingredient: pastured heritage pork.

On cooking day:

PREP
- -

Mise en place.

Take out of the fridge the amount of bacon you want to cook—and, if you have time, let it sit for about 20 minutes to get to room temperature.

Line a serving plate with paper towels to drain the bacon after cooking.

2 cooking options: 1) bake in oven or 2) fry in skillet

OPTION 1 – OVEN
Preheat oven to 300º F.

In a **baking pan** or two, arrange side by side without overlapping
- ◆ The bacon slices you want to cook

Bake about 25 minutes, until done to your liking.

Transfer the bacon to the paper-toweled plate and let it drain.

Option 2 – SKILLET
In a cold *skillet*, arrange the bacon slices side by side without overlapping.

Turn the heat on low and put a **bacon press** on top of the bacon to prevent curling. If you don't have a bacon press, use a pot that's smaller than your skillet, bottom of the pot on the bacon. Weigh the pot down with water if necessary. Cook about 3 minutes.

Check the bacon, and when the cooked side is ready, turn the slices over and press them down as before. Cook another few minutes, until done to your liking. If the bacon is not as crisp or brown as you like, keep it on the skillet a bit longer without the press until it's as you like it.

---

[20] A 24-hour marinade in a salty or acidic medium is necessary to prevent a negative reaction in our blood to unmarinated pork. (See Beverly Rubik, "How Does Pork Prepared in Various Ways Affect the Blood?" in *Wise Traditions,* Fall 2011, p27.

When done, transfer the bacon to the paper-toweled plate to drain, and pour the bacon grease into a mason jar. Repeat the cooking process until all the bacon you want to cook is done.

SERVE

Remove the paper towel and serve.

Bacon is a great accompaniment to eggs, and it can also be chopped into bite-sized pieces to liven up green salads or steamed veggies.

Enjoy!

STORE

Transfer the bacon grease to another **mason jar**, straining it to remove the brown bits from the bacon. Use the grease to cook eggs or flavor steamed veggies. It lasts about a month in the fridge.

Bacon and its grease freeze well. To defrost, move to fridge at least one day before using.

Any Liver with Almost-Caramelized Onions

This is a quick, affordable, and delicious way to get lots of nutrition! Start with the onions, because the liver cooks more quickly. You can cook the liver in the same skillet, where the cooking fat that has been infused with a divine onion flavor.

SERVES 4

When to start: 25 minutes before enjoying
Hands-on time: 20 minutes
Stove time: 25 minutes

PREP

Mise en place.

Heat on medium low a *9 or 10-inch skillet*.

Peel, cut in half, and slice thinly
   ♦ **1 large Onion, red or yellow**

Cut to separate the lobes of chicken livers
   ♦ **1 pound Chicken livers**
Or use **calf's liver** (no prep needed).

COOK

Add to and dissolve in the heated skillet
   ♦ **1 Tb Schmaltz (chicken fat), lard, taste-free coconut oil, or ghee**

Add, cover pan, and cook to soften (about 10 minutes), stirring occasionally
   ♦ The sliced **Onion**

Transfer onion to the serving plate or to individual meal plates, and keep warm.

Turn up the skillet heat to medium high and add
   ♦ **1 Tb Fat (same kind used for the onion)**

THE LIVER
Cook the liver, flipping to brown, about 4 minutes total. When done, the liver should still be pink in the middle. Overdone livers become like cardboard.

Transfer the liver to a serving dish or individual meal plates with the onions.

Deglaze the pan and Add
- ½ cup or more Chicken broth, water, sherry, or red wine

Scrape up the flavorful bits sticking to the bottom.

Cook until the liquid is reduced and syrupy.

Optional:
Turn off the heat and add
- 1-2 Tb Butter and/or heavy cream

SERVE
- -
Pour sauce over the livers and serve.

Enjoy!

Chicken Adobo, National Dish

Adobo is so widely eaten in the Philippines; it's considered the national dish. You can make it with any meat or seafood, but chicken adobo was the favorite in our family—my mom made it often.

Here's her recipe, except that she used a regular pot and I use an Instant Pot, which hadn't yet been invented. You can also use a regular slow cooker plus skillet for browning if you don't have an Instant Pot, whose only advantage is dirtying only one pot to both brown the chicken and cook it.

SERVES 4-8

When to start: 1 hour to 9 ½ hours before enjoying
Hands-on time: 12-25 minutes
Stove time: 40 minutes to 9 hours 10 minutes

PREP

Mise en place.

Crush, peel, slice, or **smash** and let sit for 10 minutes
  ♦ **1 head (10 cloves) Garlic**

Prep the chicken

OPTION 1:
Rinse and dry
  ♦ **4-8 pounds Thighs**

OPTION 2:
Cut up into pieces (drumsticks, thighs, wings, breasts)
  ♦ **1-2 Chickens**

Separate the carcass and wing tips to use for making broth. If using 2 chickens, you could save the breasts to make nuggets for another meal.

COOK

Heat in a *skillet* on medium or in an *Instant Pot* on sauté
  ♦ **1 Tb Chicken or duck fat, ghee, or no taste coconut oil**

Sauté the sliced garlic a couple of minutes until soft.

Add the chicken and brown.

Transfer chicken and garlic to slow cooker or turn Instant Pot on Slow Cook. Add
- **¼ - ½ cup Red wine or apple cider vinegar**
- **¼ - ½ cup Coconut Aminos**
- **1-2 tsp Salt**
- **1-2 Tb Whole peppercorns** (put in a tea basket for easy removal[21])
- **2-3 large Bay leaves, creased**
- **1-2 cups Poultry broth or water**

Optional:
- **Generous sprinkling Paprika**

Cook until the chicken is falling off the bone:
- Slow cook 6-9 hours *or*
- Pressure cook 30-40 minutes
- Simmer 40-60 minutes

TIP: If time is short, skip browning the garlic and chicken, throw everything in the pot, and cook until it's done.

SERVE

The adobo is ready when the chicken is falling off the bone.

Remove the bay leaves and the peppercorns in the tea basket.

Serve the adobo over Beats Rice, spooning the juice over all.

Accompany with a cooked green vegetable.

Enjoy!

---

[21] To prevent diners' shock when they bite into a peppercorn.

Exploder Chicken

You'll need an Instant Pot or pressure cooker for this dish. But *only two ingredients* and *five minutes of hands-on time!*

I've always been wary of the intense force of a pressure cooker.[22] I ignored the Pressure Cook setting of my Instant Pot until one day … I was in a huge hurry, and all I had to make for dinner was a raw pastured chicken that had been sitting in my fridge several days. Into the Instant Pot it went with Himalayan salt[23] and a couple of quarts of farmer-made pastured poultry broth. Invoking all the cooking gods, I hit Pressure Cook.

Thirty-five minutes later, there it was—the most succulent chicken falling off the bone I had ever had. We named it Exploder Chicken—not because it actually exploded, but as a tribute to my Instant Pot—which I will forever call The Exploder. The name now evokes awesome power rather than unfounded fear.

SERVES 4-10

When to start:	45 minutes before enjoying
Hands-on time:	5 minutes
Stove time:	35 minutes

PREP

Mise en place.

◆ Rinse **1 Whole chicken**

Sprinkle chicken with
◆ **To taste Salt**

---

[22] I tell this story also in the second of this book trio, *Crazy Eating in the Land of Foodlike Substances.*
[23] I did not add the usual herbs and spices, because I had just started my Carnivore Diet experiment and was off all plant foods.

Optional:
- **To taste Spices and herbs of your choice**

COOK

Put the whole chicken in the ***Instant Pot*** and select Pressure Cook, 35 minutes.
- **Add 2 quarts Chicken stock or water**

When done, release the pressure per machine directions.

Let chicken rest about 10 minutes.

SERVE

Transfer chicken to meat cutting board and separate pieces to serve. The chicken should be melting in your mouth.

Enjoy!

Moroccan Chicken Tagine[24]

A fire-engine red ceramic Emile Henri tagine sits prominently on my stove, even when not in use. It's not just for cooking—it brightens my kitchen and makes me happy.

A tagine is a vessel used to cook stews in North Africa—lamb, beef, or chicken, with potatoes, other veggies, onion, garlic, and regional spices. This recipe is our version of Moroccan chicken tagine based on ideas from Chef Traci,[25] Christine Benlafquih of *The Spruce Eats*,[26] Melissa Clark of the *New York Times*,[27] and Analida of ethnicspoon.com.[28] It is a one-pot meal cooked slowly and eaten fast—because it is so tender, delicious, and comforting.

Tagine

"Tagine" is used to refer to the recipe, as well as to the cooking vessel. A tagine layers meat, veggies, and spices, with oil and water or stock to yield a rich, flavorful sauce after slow cooking. Its secret is its cover's conical shape, which returns droplets of condensed steam back to the food, preserving its moistness. If you don't have a tagine, cook your tagine in a Dutch oven or other big, heavy pot.

IMPORTANT TO DO BEFORE COOKING DAY

1. If using a *new* **tagine**, season it:
   - Soak the tagine in cold water for at two hours or more; overnight is fine.
   - Dry the tagine. If it is unglazed, rub the interior and exterior with olive oil.
   - Place the tagine in a *cold* oven and turn it to 300° F. (Do not place the tagine in a heated oven as it may crack.) Leave in 300° F oven for two hours.
   - Turn off the oven and leave the tagine to cool *completely* in the oven.

---

[24] Beef, pork or lamb are ok too. Just increase the cooking time—taste and adjust.

[25] At a cooking class in Berkeley, California some time in 2017.

[26] An excellent illustrated step-by-step description of how to cook a tagine. See https://www.thespruceeats.com/cooking-in-a-moroccan-tagine-steps-2395002

[27] Who French-ifies tagine cooking, https://cooking.nytimes.com/guides/36-how-to-make-tagine

[28] Who passes on a recipe from a Moroccan friend, https://ethnicspoon.com/moroccan-chicken-tagine/

- Wash the cooled tagine by hand and coat the interior with olive oil before using or storing.
- When cooking, use *low* heat and place a *heat diffuser* between the stove top or flame and the tagine. (Authentic Moroccan tagines may crack if subjected to high heat.) You need to season a tagine only once! It ensures that you can enjoy easy cooking with the tagine for many, many years.

2. Hand wash your tagine after using and let it dry thoroughly. If unglazed, lightly coat the interior with olive oil before storing. Store your tagine slightly ajar so air can circulate.

3. If you think you'll make tagines again, make a large batch of the spices and store in a cool dark place. I call this my Moroccan readymix. Use any 4 or more of these spices, especially paprika, coriander, cinnamon, and garlic.

For **half a cup of spice mix**

- ◆ **3 ½ Tb Sweet paprika**
- ◆ **3 Tb Ground coriander**
- ◆ **1 Tb Turmeric**
- ◆ **1 Tb Ginger**
- ◆ **½ Tb Cardamom**
- ◆ **2 tsp Cinnamon**
- ◆ **1 tsp Garlic powder**
- ◆ **Pinch Saffron**

4. Aim to salt the chicken one or two days before cooking. But salting any time before cooking is better than none. One day before is ideal, more than two is too much.[29]

When to start: If your tagine is new, 8½ hours before enjoying; if seasoned, 2 ½ hours
Hands-on time: 30 minutes
Stove time: 2 hours

PREP

Mise en place.

Peel and **slice** into 1/8" rounds
- ◆ **1-2 Onions, yellow or red**

---
[29] Samin Nosrat, *Salt Fat Acid Heat*, page 32. Samin reports that meat salted more than two days tends to be dry and taste like cured meat. If salted less than overnight, the superior flavor of overnight salting is noticeable.

Arrange the onion rounds in an overlapping layer or two, to cover the bottom of the tagine.

Peel and slice, press or scatter whole on top of the onions
- **4-5 cloves Garlic**

Wash, peel, and cut all or some of these veggies and set them aside
- **2 Zucchini: Cut lengthwise in half or quarters**
- **3 Carrots: Peeled and cut lengthwise in half**

Optional:
- **1 Bell pepper: Cut into half rounds**
- **Handful Green olives**
- **To taste Preserved lemons**
- **Several sprigs Parsley, for garnish**

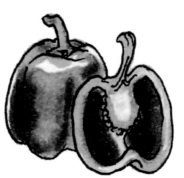

green bell pepper

Take out of the package and rinse
- **8 Chicken thighs**

OR cut a whole chicken into 10 pieces:
- 2 drumsticks, 2 thighs, 2 wings, 4 breast pieces.

If you don't have a readymix of the tagine spices, mix a batch now, making more than you need, for future use.
(See list of spices above.)

Season the onions with
- **1 tsp Salt**
- **1 Tb Moroccan readymix**

Douse the onions and garlic with
- **¼ cup Olive oil**

Mound the chicken pieces on top of the onion and garlic, in the center of the *tagine*.
Arrange the prepped veggies around the chicken and sprinkle over the veggies.
- **1 tsp Salt**

Sprinkle over the veggies and chicken
- **2 Tb Moroccan readymix**

Douse the chicken and veggies with
- **¼ cup Olive oil**

COOK

Put a **heat diffuser** on the burner you will be using and put the tagine on the diffuser.

Add to the tagine
- **1½ cups Chicken stock or water or a combo**

Turn the heat to medium low and let the tagine reach a low to medium simmer (takes up to half an hour).

Cook the tagine about 1½ hours, checking after an hour.

SERVE

Arrange a piece or two of chicken and some of each vegetable on each plate, spooning the sauce over all.

Can accompany with Legal Bread, Beats Rice or Could Be Mashed Potato to soak up the rich flavors of your tagine.

Enjoy a taste of Morocco!

Fish

**Eat only if it comes from
non-polluted waters**

10-Minute Fish Fillet

This is a no-frills, fast, and delicious way to cook a fillet of any fish. It's the only dish Kip, one of my clients, cooks—his other half cooks everything else. But he's cooked this several times a month for years.

SERVES 2

When to start: 10 minutes before enjoying
Hands-on time: 8 minutes
Stove time: 6 minutes

PREP

Mise en place.

Rinse and plump
- **2 4-ounce fillets of wild New Zealand salmon[30] or other wild fish**

Hold each fillet under filtered running water and gently shake and pat the fish as the water runs over it, about a minute.

Place fillets side by side on ***wax paper***[31] on counter, skin side down.

Sprinkle generously with
- **Salt and pepper**
- **Garlic powder**
- **Onion powder**

(I mix garlic powder and onion powder together 50-50 and keep a bottle of the mix handy.)

---

[30] I eat only Southern Hemisphere salmon now, because I feel that seafood from the polluted Northern Hemisphere oceans is no longer safe. I have found a source of beautiful fresh New Zealand salmon: Hapuku Fish in Market Hall, Oakland, California.
[31] Counterfold wax paper comes in convenient sheets and saves time tearing it off a roll. Use one sheet per fillet.

COOK

Heat on medium high *a skillet that just fits the fish,* and add

- **1 Tb Ghee or taste-free coconut oil** (If you prefer olive oil, heat skillet on medium or medium low to reduce nutrient damage.)

When the fat starts shimmering, carefully lay the fish skin side up in the pan and cook the flesh side to golden, about 2-3 minutes.

Flip the fillets and turn the heat down to medium low. If the fish is uneven in thickness, move the pan so that the thin side of the fillets is away from direct heat.

Cover the pan and cook about 2-6 minutes depending on the thickness of the fillet and the degree of doneness you like. Thin fillets like sole or snapper are done quickly. *Salmon*, halibut, or other thicker fillets need more.

It might take a few tries to determine the amount of time for medium rare salmon, for example, or soft, juicy sole. Stay with it and your patience and precision will pay off in tender, juicy, fragrant, golden brown fish fillets.

SERVE

Serve plain or over Beats Rice or Could Be Mashed Potatoes, and/or a fresh green salad.

Garnish with a lemon wedge.

Enjoy!

Poached Salmon

Inspired by a recipe created by Tamar Cohen, nutritionist and owner of Triholistic Nutrition. Poached salmon can be used in many ways—salad, soup, snack …

SERVES 4

When to start:	40 minutes before enjoying
Hands-on time:	10 minutes
Stove time:	10-15 minutes

salmon

PREP

Mise en place.

Slice into 1/8" rounds
- 1 Lemon

Poaching Liquid:
In *a braising pan*, add
- 4 cups Water
- The sliced Lemon
- 3 Parsley sprigs
- 2 tsp Whole black peppercorns
- 1 tsp Salt

lemon

Bring the liquid to a gentle boil.

Taste and adjust the seasoning if necessary.

THE SALMON

Gently slide into the poaching liquid

- **1 lb Salmon fillets, preferably with skin (for added taste)**

Cover and cook 5-10 minutes depending on the thickness of the fillets. Important not to overcook.

With a *slotted spoon*, remove the fillets and set aside to cool.

When cool, remove the skin and break the fillets into bite-sized pieces with your hands.

Save poaching liquid. Can freeze it for future use in soup or poaching another round of fillets.

SERVE

Enjoy the poached salmon as-is or with a dollop of Mayo Verde (see recipe in Sides, Spreads ...) and a salad on the side.

OR make a salmon salad (see recipe) ...

OR drop the salmon into any hot broth or soup for just a few minutes to heat it, and you can have a scrumptious fish soup in minutes.

Enjoy!

Salmon Salad

Also based on nutritionist and athlete Tamar Cohen's voluminous recipe repertoire. Gives you a dish you can enjoy at home for a fraction of the cost at a restaurant.

SERVES 4

When to start: 10 minutes before enjoying
Hands-on time: 10 minutes
Stove time: 0 minutes

PREP

Mise en place.

Dice
- ◆ **1 Avocado**

Chop
- ◆ **¼ cup Red onion**
- ◆ **½ cup Parsley or dill** and set aside half for garnish

parsley

Juice
- ◆ **½ Lemon**

THE SALAD

In a ***large bowl***, gently combine
All Prepped ingredients, being careful not to mash the avocado
- ◆ **1 lb. Poached salmon**
- ◆ **2 Tb Olive oil**
- ◆ **½ tsp Black pepper**

To taste
- ◆ **Salt**

SERVE

Garnish the salad with the herbs you set aside.

Optional:
Pass around
- ◆ **1 cup Mayo Verde** (see recipe in Sides, Spreads ...)

Enjoy!

Instant Sardines

Sardines are affordable for almost anyone. Even the most expensive sardines (in a glass jar) are less than half the cost of the cheapest fresh salmon (at a superstore). Yet they are delicious and can look as enticing on a plate as salmon.

Replace the salmon in the Salmon Salad with sardines and you will have another exquisite salad! With Instant Sardines, you can enjoy awesomely nutritious food even when you have no time to cook.

This recipe is based on the unique creation of Tamar Cohen, my nutrition club colleague and dear friend.

SERVES 2

When to start: 5 minutes before enjoying
Hands-on time: 5 minutes
Stove time: 0 minutes

PREP

Mise en place.

Drain, place in a **serving bowl** and set aside the liquids in
 ◆ **1 8-oz jar Sardines**, wild caught, in olive oil, preferably in a glass jar[32] (e.g., Ortiz brand)
 ◆ **1 cup Sauerkraut**

THE SALAD

Mix the sardines and sauerkraut together.

SERVE

Serve as-is or with lettuce.

You can also drizzle the reserved olive oil from the sardines and/or the sauerkraut juice over the salad.

Enjoy!

---

[32] To avoid chemicals in can linings that may have leached into canned sardines.

SIDES

*They make a meal complete,
often nudging out
sugar-filled desserts.*

Salads

Salads—with their skinnifying reputation—are the star of side dishes, from simple lettuces popularized by Alice Waters, to exotic Arabian tabbouleh, which is surprisingly easy to make at home. The secret is fresh ingredients with just enough dressing to make the salad sparkle.

Glistening Greens with Go-To Salad Dressing

Early in her professional cooking life, Alice Waters won a chef's competition with a simple, exquisite one-ingredient salad she dressed simply at the last minute with red wine vinegar, olive oil, black pepper, and salt. She carried the living lettuce with her, its roots still in soil, so it would be the freshest possible.[33]

The salad here has three ingredients without the dressing. I never tire of it, even if it's on the table several times a week.

SERVES 4

When to start: 10 minutes before enjoying
Hands-on time: 10 minutes
Stove time: 0 minutes

PREP

Take out a **salad bowl** and add to it the ingredients as they are prepared.

Separate the leaves, wash, **spin dry**, and tear into bite-sized pieces
  ◆ **1 head Living butter lettuce**[34]

butter
lettuce

---

[33] Now supermarkets carry basil, mint, and lettuce living in their plastic packages, roots planted in soil.
[34] My grocery store sells heads of lettuce packed with their roots still embedded in soil.

Harvest[35] (or buy), wash, spin dry, and tear into pieces if leaves are too big
- **2 handfuls Arugula**

Optional:
Slice thinly
- **½ Onion, any color (or 2-3 scallion stalks)**

Sprinkle and drizzle over the greens
- **Several grinds Salt**
- **4 Tb Go-To Salad Dressing** (see recipe)

Toss with hands, ***tongs,*** or ***two forks***, taste, and add more dressing as needed.

SERVE

Serve on salad or dinner plates. Delight in the sight of the glistening leaves

Enjoy!

---

[35] I have organic arugula growing in a pot on my deck.

Go-To Salad Dressing

I use this dressing for almost all salads. It's based on Alice Waters' recipe for her "garden salad" in *The Art of Simple Foods*, page 51, with a few personal tweaks. The recipe makes more than the amount for immediate use, so that salad making can be quick. When I run out of dressing and have no time to make more, I just sprinkle each ingredient on the leaves using my garlic and onion readymix powder instead of fresh. Not as wonderful, but still good …

Adjust the ingredients until you have a dressing you love. Note the final amounts so you can duplicate it and enjoy an awesome dressing every time.

MAKES ¾ to 1¼ cup

When to start: 5 minutes before enjoying
Hands-on time: 5 minutes
Stove time: 0 minutes

PREP

Mise en place.

Peel, *slice* and remove the green stem in the center from
- **1 clove Garlic**

Pound the garlic to a fine paste with a **mortar and pestle**, OR *press* it into a **small bowl**. In the mortar or small bowl, mix together the garlic with
- **¼ cup Red wine vinegar,**[36] **traditional balsamic vinegar, or lemon juice**
- **½ tsp Salt**
- **To taste Black pepper**

Taste and adjust, knowing that the flavor will be softened when you add olive oil.

Whisk in
- **½-1 cup Olive oil**

Double the recipe, or more, for future use. This dressing stays good at least a couple of weeks.

Extra-virgin olive oil

Enjoy!

---

[36] Red wine vinegar does not contain any alcohol. It contains trace amounts of nutrients, such as the minerals magnesium, calcium, potassium, and iron; antioxidants; and a substance from grape skin that may prevent damage to blood vessels (resveratrol).

Four Variations on Cucumber Salad

Cucumber salads are quick and easy. We don't have to wash and spin cucumbers like we do lettuce. We don't even have to peel them if time is short. With a mandoline, a big one is sliced in less than a minute and the peel is unnoticeable.

"Half-peeling"—leaving lengthwise strips of peel on the cucumber—gives an interesting pattern to the slices and takes less time than complete peeling. Cucumbers are bland and fresh tasting, so you can give them the zing you like— California, Hungarian, kefir or Japanese.

1. CUKES CALIFORNIA

SERVES 4

When to start: 10 minutes before enjoying
Hands-on time: 10 minutes
Stove time: 0 minutes

PREP

Mise en place.

Peel, cut into bite-sized cubes,
and add to *serving bowl*
- 1 English or Persian/Armenian Cucumber
- 1 Avocado

avocado

Chop or mince and add to bowl
- 2 Tb Cilantro or basil
- 1 clove Garlic
- 1 stalk Scallion, including roots

Mix in
- 1 Tb Lime juice (1/2 to 1 lime)
- To taste Salt
- To taste Black pepper

Optional:
- To taste Garlic and onion readymix powder

Enjoy!

2. HUNGARIAN[37] CUCUMBER SALAD

SERVES 4

When to start: 10 minutes before enjoying
Hands-on time: 10 minutes
Stove time: 0 minutes

PREP

Mise en place.

Wash and slice with a *mandoline* or *knife*
- **1 English[38] or Persian/Armenian[39] cucumber**
- **1 White onion, small to medium**

Mince
- **2 Tb Fresh herb: dill or mint leaves**

Toss cucumber, onion, and herb together.

Sprinkle over the cucumber and toss after adding each ingredient
- **3 Tb White wine vinegar[40]**
- **3 Tb Olive oil**
- **1 tsp Salt**

mint

Enjoy!

---

[37] "Hungarian" refers to the ingredient mix in the salad rather than the type of cucumber.
[38] English cucumbers are a variety of cucumber bred to eliminate the slight bitterness, large seeds, and tough skin of regular slicing cucumbers. They are also about double the length of a regular cucumber.
[39] Persian cucumbers are also known as Armenian cucumbers. They are similar to English cucumbers (previous footnote) except they often have light green skin and are ribbed.
[40] I use Napa Valley Naturals organic white wine vinegar, in a glass bottle.

3. KEFIR CUCUMBER[41]

Serves 4
When to start: 45 minutes before enjoying
Hands-on time: 10 minutes
Stove time: 0 minutes

PREP

Mise en place.

Peel or half-peel[42]
   ◆ **1 English or Persian/Armenian cucumber**

Halve the cucumber crosswise, then halve lengthwise (to create half-moons), then slice with a **mandoline** or **knife**.

Or cut into bite-sized cubes and add to serving bowl.

Toss cucumber with a pinch of salt, allow to sit for 10 mins to extract liquid, then drain.

Mince and add
   ◆ **2-4 sprigs Mint or dill** (1 heaping tablespoon minced)

Optional:
   ◆ **Jalapeño** (minced) **or a pinch of cayenne**

Peel, ***press***,[43] and add
   ◆ **1 clove Garlic**

Stir in:
   ◆ **1 Tb Olive oil**
   ◆ **¾ cup Homemade kefir or yogurt**
   ◆ **Or ½ cup Sour cream**

Let sit at least 30 minutes to meld flavors. ***Enjoy!***

---

[41] Based on Alice Waters' "Cucumber-Yogurt Sauce" recipe in *The Art of Simple Food*, page 232.

[42] "Half-peel" is leaving lengthwise strips of peel to create a pattern of green and white on the outside of the cucumber

[43] Garlic press available at Amazon. I use the crusher model with handles, rather than the rocker.

4. JAPANESE CUCUMBER SALAD (*SUNOMONO*)

No worries, the dressing in Crazy Eating sunomono has no sugar.

PREP

In a **small bowl**, combine dressing ingredients and set aside
- ◆ **2 tsp Rice vinegar**[44]
- ◆ **2 tsp Mirin** (Japanese sweet rice cooking wine)
- ◆ **3 tsp Coconut Aminos**[45]

Wash, half-*peel*, slice (with a **mandoline** if possible), and place in a **serving bowl**
- ◆ **1 Japanese cucumber**[46]

Toss the cucumber with
- ◆ **¼ tsp Salt**

Let it sit about 10 minutes to extract water, then drain and squeeze the water out.

Pour on the dressing and toss.

Sprinkle over the cucumber
- ◆ **A Handful of Sesame seeds,** preferably toasted[47]

sesame seeds

Enjoy!

---

[44] Make sure the rice vinegar has no added sugar, e.g., Kikkoman is in a glass bottle.
[45] Coconut Aminos, made by Coconut Secret, is a substitute for soy sauce. It's a bit sweeter and not as intense.
[46] A Japanese cucumber (aka suyo cucumber) is shorter than an English cucumber and does not contain any developed seeds. It is crisp and has a bright melon-like flavor.
[47] In a small skillet over medium heat, toast sesame seeds until fragrant, 3-5 minutes.

Mom's Persian Salad

PREP

Mise en place.

Add each ingredient to the serving bowl as it is prepped.

1. Peel and dice into bite-sized cubes
   - **1 Red onion**
   - **1 Persian/Armenian or English Cucumber**

2. Seed (cut in half and gently squeeze) and dice
   - **2 Tomatoes**

3. Mince (or use dried)
   - **2 Tb Fresh mint leaves (1 Tb dried)**
   - **2 tsp Fresh dill leaves (1 tsp dried)**

4. Add and toss after adding each ingredient
   - **1 Tb Lemon or lime juice** (1 lemon or lime)
   - **3 Tb Olive oil**
   - **1+ tsp Ground sumac** [48]

OR
   - **2+tsp Li'l Readymix** (see recipe in **Accents and Sauces**)

   - **1+ tsp Salt and pepper**

Enjoy!

Sumac

---

[48] Sumac is a deep red Middle Eastern herb that imparts a subtle lemony taste. It is commonly used in Persian cuisine.

Wheat-Free Tabbouleh (Aka Parsley Salad[49])

Tabbouleh comes to us from the Middle East, where it has been eaten for centuries, since the Middle Ages. It's made with a lot of raw herbs and veggies, but common tabbouleh also has a ton of cracked wheat, called bulgur.

This recipe eliminates the wheat and offers just the fresh, nourishing plants—more nutrition, less preparation.

SERVES 6-8

When to start: 1½ hour before enjoying
Hands-on time: 10-15 minutes
Stove time: 0 minutes

PREP

Mise en place.

Take out a **large bowl** to put all prepped ingredients in as they are prepped.

Core and ***dice***
- ◆ **1 Medium cucumber**
- ◆ **1 Medium tomato or bell pepper** of any color

Chop finely by hand or pulse in a ***food processor***

- ◆ **1 bunch Parsley** (1½ cups chopped)
- ◆ **½ bunch Mint (1/3** cup chopped)
- ◆ **3 large stalks Scallions (1** cup chopped**)**
- ◆ **or spring/red onion**

Optional:
(especially if you have it left over)
- ◆ **1 cup Beats Rice, cooked** (to replace the bulgur in common tabbouleh)

Juice
- ◆ **1 Lemon** (3 Tb juice)

---

[49] Based on Alice Waters' recipe for tabbouleh in *The Art of Simple Food*, p. 248

Add and mix in
- **3 Tb Olive oil**
- **1/2 tsp Salt**

Taste and adjust the salt, olive oil, or lemon juice.

Let the tabbouleh rest about an hour.

Optional:
Wash and separate the leaves of
- **1 head Butter or iceberg lettuce**—for use as serving "cups"

SERVE

Serve with a main course of meat, chicken, or fish.

Or, spoon the tabbouleh into lettuce leaves or small bowls as a first course.

Optional:
Pass around chopped tomato, Serrano chilies, hot sauce, or olive oil.

Enjoy!

Cooked Veggies

Cooked veggies often remain on plates waiters whisk away to make room for dessert. I hope the veggie recipes here woo you into enjoying them at home.

One Recipe, Many Veggies

Prep the veggies, season, steam, add your favorite fat, and serve. Voila! This step sequence works for all 5% vegetables—those that have no more than 5% carbohydrate, listed in Nitty Gritty 1. Dressing steamed veggies with a fat yields many benefits over cooking the veggies in fat. We get the rich flavor and texture of butter, olive oil, sesame, and other oils without possible damage to the oils when heating. Nutrients remain intact and the veggies are plump and moist.

If you already steam vegetables as a matter of course, skip to the end, where you'll find a reminder to douse your steamed veggies with a qualified fat. The fat transforms the veggies from obligatory to yummy.

SERVES the number you want
When to start: 20 minutes before enjoying
Hands-on time: 10 minutes
Stove time: 10 minutes

PREP
Mise en place.

Bring saved steaming water[50] or new water to a boil in a **steamer pot** over medium high heat. Wash and peel the veggies, de-stem, and/or slice or tear. (Tools: **vegetable peeler** or **paring knife, chef's knife** and **cutting board** or **mandoline**.)

COOK
Put the veggies in the **steamer basket** and sprinkle to taste with
- **Salt and any powdered seasonings you like**, such as garlic and onion powder or a readymix

Steam for about 4 to 8 minutes or until veggies are fork tender.

SERVE
Transfer the veggies to a serving dish and toss generously with any *qualified* fat:
- **Olive oil, Butter, compound butter,[51] or ghee**
- **Walnut or sesame oil**
- **Any saved animal fat, e.g. lard, schmaltz, or tallow**

Taste and adjust seasoning if necessary. ***Enjoy!***

---

[50] After steaming veggies or any other food, I save the steaming water in a mason jar in the fridge to use for future steaming.
[51] See Garlic Butter and Wild Mushroom Butter recipes.

Broccoli[52] Soup with Sautéed Garlic[53]

This is the dish I usually bring to potlucks. I pour it into quart mason jars that I transport in a canvas wine carrier nestled in an insulated bag that also holds a ladle, olive oil bottle, and sautéed garlic jar. My serving tureen is an All Clad silver stainless steel Dutch oven with domed cover in which I can easily reheat the soup if necessary. The oooh's and aaaah's keep me bringing this soup to the next potluck and the next …

SERVES 8

When to start: 40-45 minutes ahead
Hands-on time: 15-20 minutes
Stove time: 20 minutes

PREP

Mise en place.

---

[52] You can use cauliflower instead of broccoli.

[53] Based on a cauliflower soup recipe in *Real Simple*, January 2013

Peel and *slice*, then set aside
- ◆ **12 cloves Garlic**

Clean and *chop* into bite-sized pieces
- ◆ **½ cup Onion, any color** (1 medium onion)
- ◆ **4 cups Broccoli** (2 bunches)

Optional:
- ◆ **1 cup Celery**
- ◆ **1 cup Carrots**
- ◆ **2 Tb Parsley leaves**

COOK

In a *large pot* or *Instant Pot*, heat on medium
- ◆ **2-3 Tb Fat: Duck,** chicken or pork, ghee, or taste-free coconut oil

Add the sliced garlic and sauté until golden, 2-3 mins. Transfer the garlic to a dish to pass around when the soup is served.

Add and sauté the chopped onion, about five minutes.

Stir in
- ◆ The chopped broccoli
- ◆ The chopped carrots
- ◆ The chopped celery, if using
- ◆ **2 quarts Bone broth,** including the natural fat

  OR
- ◆ **1½ quarts Broth**
- ◆ **2 cups Coconut milk**
- ◆ **¾ tsp or to taste Salt**

broccoli

Optional:
- ◆ **2 tsp Heidi's Peak Performance spice mix** (garlic, onion, rosemary, thyme, sage., fennel)

Bring to a boil, lower heat and simmer until the broccoli is tender, 15-20 mins.

Cool the soup a bit and puree it in a regular *blender* OR with an *immersion blender*.

IMPORTANT: If your blender pitcher is glass or metal, it's ok for the soup to be pretty hot when you puree it. If your blender pitcher is plastic, cool the soup down to room temp before blending to avoid plasticizers leaching into the soup.

Blend for just a few seconds on high if you like a coarse texture, longer if you like it smooth.

Taste and adjust seasonings as necessary.

SERVE

Ladle the soup into serving bowls and pass around olive oil and the sautéed garlic.

Enjoy!

"Starches!"

Bread, rice and potatoes are, let's face it, fattening. Yet, they're always first on the table in restaurants; they're indispensable for traditional sandwiches, and they're a way to fill an empty stomach with minimal expense. Instead of avoiding them, we suggest ways to make them without interfering with fat-burning goals.

Beats Rice

Made with cauliflower, it is known as cauliflower rice in Paleo circles and among low-carb eaters. It was first named "cauliflower couscous" back in 1998 by its creator Ben Ford,[54] a Los Angeles chef who has cooked with California star chefs Alice Waters and Paul Bertolli. Cauliflower rice took off when New York chef Eric Ripert put it on his popular TV show *Avec Eric*. I like to call it Beats Rice, so it remains mysterious till the first delicious bite.

cauliflower

SERVES 6-8

When to start: 25 minutes before enjoying
Hands-on time: 15 minutes
Stove time: 10 minutes

PREP

Mise en place.

Take out a **Dutch oven** or **large pot** to put all prepped ingredients in.

Peel, **chop**, and add to pot
 ♦ **5-9 Garlic cloves** (remove green stem inside)

Mince and add to pot other fresh herbs to yield 1/3 cup total (or use ½ the quantity of powders), e.g.
 ♦ **Thyme**
 ♦ **Basil**
 ♦ **Sage**
 ♦ **Chives**—reserve some for garnish
 ♦ **Parsley**—for garnish

Cut off the florets, discarding the stalk and leaves of
 ♦ **1 head Cauliflower**

Process the florets in a **food processor** with a regular blade, pulsing until the florets reach the size of rice grains—less than a minute. Add to pot.

---

[54] Son of actor Harrison Ford

COOK

Add to the Dutch oven/pot
- **1quart Duck or chicken stock**
- **1 tsp Salt**
- **To taste Black pepper**
- **1 tsp Garlic powder**
- **1 tsp Onion powder**

Optional:
- **2 tsp Your own readymix spices**

Cover and cook until cauliflower is tender, about 10 minutes.

Taste and adjust.

SERVE

Transfer the "rice" to a serving dish, sprinkle and toss with
- The minced garnishing herbs
- **Olive oil**

Enjoy—as a side, or a foil underneath your main dish.

P.S. Beats Rice can easily be made into **Cauliflower Soup with Toasted Garlic** by adding more broth and sautéing the peeled cloves of a head of garlic to pass around when the soup is served.

See the Broccoli Soup recipe in this section, which works for cauliflower too.

Enjoy!

Could-Be Mashed Potato

If you liked Beats Rice, you'll love this. The secret isn't the cauliflower; it's the butter and cream! By now you know how good quality fat is for us, so we welcome opportunities to eat it, especially when it tastes as good as raw butter and cream.

SERVES 4 to 8

When to start: 25 minutes before enjoying
Hands-on time: 15 minutes
Stove time: 10 minutes

PREP

Mise en place.

***Peel**, **cut** in half lengthwise, de-stem, and let sit about 10 minutes[55]*
- **5-10 cloves Garlic**

Separate into florets
- **1-2 heads Cauliflower**

COOK

***Steam** the cauliflower and garlic for 15 minutes or until tender, so a fork can easily pass through.*

Optional: Mince fresh herbs
- **1/3 to ½ cup Basil, chives, scallions, mint, parsley, etc.**

Put in *food processor, blender, or large bowl*
- The steamed Cauliflower and garlic
- **1 tsp Salt**
- **1 Tb Butter**
- **2 Tb Heavy cream**

***Blend** (or mash with a **fork or potato masher**) to mashed potato consistency—smooth or chunky, as you prefer.*

Taste and adjust seasonings, butter, and cream.

SERVE

Transfer to serving dish and add meat or vegetable juices if available.

***Enjoy** as a side or a foil underneath your main entrée!*

---

[55] To release its active ingredient, allicin.

Legal Bread

It's the wheat that makes bread unhealthy and addictive. Replace the wheat with a benign ingredient—like coconut flour—and you're home free.

Coconut flour contains a fraction of the carbs in wheat flour[56] and none of the anti-nutrients that may interfere with mineral absorption and promote inflammation in the digestive tract.

Most keto or Paleo bread recipes call for almond flour. So, why does this cookbook use *coconut* flour? Because much less flour is required to make coconut flour bread and, unlike almonds or other nuts, coconut is not a common allergen.

Legal Bread is definitely not a crunchy baguette, but it's wonderful with gobs of butter or a chunk of cheese. And no need to knead dough, or wait for it to rise. The added seeds do give Legal Bread a bit of crunch. The seeds (suggested by the creator of the Wholesome Yum blog Maya Kampf) neutralize the sweet coconut taste, and make it possible for Crazy Eaters who are watching their weight to enjoy a roast beef or turkey sandwich.

MAKES one loaf about 8½" x 4½"

When to start:	1 hr 10 min-1 hr 25 min before enjoying
Hands-on time:	10 minutes
Stove time:	60-75 minutes

PREP

Mise en place.

- -

Grease with butter or line a **9" x 5" loaf pan** with **parchment paper**. If you use parchment, let the paper hang over the long side of the pan a couple of inches or so, to allow you to use it to lift the finished loaf out of the pan.

Pre-heat oven to 350° F.

Melt
  ◆ **¾ cup (1½ stick or 12 Tb) Butter or coconut oil**

---

[56] Wheat flour has 12 times the net carbs in coconut flour. Especially for weight loss, net carbs need to be as low as possible.

In a *large bowl*, combine
- ◆ **1 cup Coconut flour**
- ◆ **1 ¼ cup Seeds: any you like: sunflower, pumpkin, sesame, etc.**
- ◆ **1½ Tb Baking powder**
- ◆ **1 tsp Salt**

Stir the melted butter into the dry ingredients until the mixture is crumbly and uniform.

In another large bowl, crack and beat with an *electric mixer or whisk,* until triple in volume
- ◆ **12 Eggs**

Fold the eggs into the batter and wait a few minutes for the batter to thicken.

Pour the batter into the loaf pan and round the top with your hands. If you like, sprinkle more seeds on top.

COOK

Bake the bread about 50 minutes until browned. Tent the bread with foil (to protect it from burning) and bake another 15-25 minutes, until the internal temperature is 170° F.

Let the bread cool in the pan. Run a knife along the sides of the loaf that touch the pan, then lift or slide it out of the pan.

SERVE

Transfer loaf to a cutting board, slice, slather with raw butter, and *enjoy!* (You won't even miss the jam...)

STORE

In the freezer, bread can last a very long time and still taste good. Slice it before freezing, then, each time you have a hankering for sinless bread, take the slices you want out of the freezer, put them in your toaster or 300° F oven and voila!

Enjoy!

NIBBLES

Virtuous Nibbles!

Chips

Run of the mill chips are made from starchy veggies—potato and corn—and they're often made with questionable fats. But they don't have to be … Zucchini, radish, and kale chips are equally fun—and different.

SERVES 4

When to start: 40-60 minutes before enjoying
Hands-on time: 10 minutes
Stove time: 30-50 minutes

GENERAL PROCEDURE

Mise en place.

Preheat oven to 325° F.

Line a **baking sheet/**pan (or two) with **parchment paper** and lightly grease with
  ◆ **1 Tb Ghee or coconut oil**

Wash, dry, and trim about
  ◆ **2 cups Chosen veggie**

Slice the veggie thinly—a **mandoline** makes slicing really easy. Only kale isn't sliced; it's de-stemmed and torn.

Toss with
  ◆ **1 Tb Ghee or coconut oil**

Season with
  ◆ **3 tsp Salt, pepper, and any other spices you like**

Spread the veggie pieces on the baking sheet in a single layer.

Bake 15-20 minutes, flip, then bake another 15-20 minutes—until crispy and golden.

Zucchini Chips

- Season *lightly* because they shrink a lot.
- Eat within a couple hours to enjoy the crispiness.

Kale Chips

Can add ½ Tb finely grated parmesan cheese to the seasonings.

Radish Chips

After trimming but before slicing, **steam** or bake the radishes about 15 minutes to soften.

Season with strong spices, e.g., curry, turmeric, garlic powder— to match the strong radish taste. About 2 tsp of spices to 20 radishes, plus salt and pepper.

Carrot or Jicama Fries

PREP

Mise en place.

.

Preheat oven to 325° F.

Line a **baking sheet/pan** (or two) with parchment and lightly grease with
- ◆ **1 Tb Ghee or coconut oil**

Wash, **peel**, and **cut** into French fry-shaped pieces
- ◆ **2 cups Carrots or** jicama

Toss with
- ◆ **1 Tb Ghee or coconut oil**

Season with
- ◆ **3 tsp Salt, pepper, and any other spices you like**

carrot

Spread the fries on the baking sheet in a single layer and bake 15-20 minutes until crispy and golden.

Optional:
Serve with a dipping sauce. See garlic aioli and blue cheese dip, variations of the Mayo Verde recipe, in Sensuous Spreads.

Enjoy!

Chicharrones a la Colombia

I loved chicharrones as a child and have never stopped loving their crunchy fat. Also called "pork rinds" they are fried pieces of fatty pork skin or pork belly, excellent for folks who eat keto.

Eating chicharrones as a first course instantly quells hunger pangs and lessens the urge to eat a lot. It is one of the most popular first courses at Comal, a popular Mexican restaurant in Berkeley, California.

If you gasped in horror at the thought of eating pork fat, you may want to read the section on "Go Fat" in the first book of the Crazy Eating trilogy: *Crazy Eating: What Should I Eat?...So I Never Have to Think about My Weight or Energy Again.* Or Jennifer McLagan's beautifully illustrated book *Fat: An Appreciation of a Misunderstood Ingredient, with Recipes.* Qualified animal fats (not vegetable oils) keep our bodies going strong; we can't be optimally healthy without them.

The crust of a pork belly roast (see recipe) contains crispy skin and fat, which you can chop into chicharrones. But you don't need a roast to get chicharrones. You can order them from U.S. Wellness, OR you can make them yourself!

In this recipe we crisp not only the skin, but also the strips of meat under the skin. It's the way they do it in Columbia, according to J. Kenji López-Alt[57] of Seriouseats.com. López-Alt published a guest post by columnist Chichi Wang, "The Nasty Bits: How to Make Chicharrones Recipe." It's brilliant and fairly easy …

---

[57] Kenji is a food scientist and one of the editors for Seriouseats.com. With a degree from MIT (Massachusetts Institute of Technology) and 11 years in restaurant kitchens, Kenji brings science to the kitchen in a massive book—over 900 pages—*The Food Lab. Better Cooking through Science.*

MAKES a couple of cups of chicharrones, to delight about 4 people

When to start: 1 day before (or at least 1 hour before) cooking
Hands-on time: 40 minutes
Seasoning soak time: 1 day
Stove time: 2-4 hours

PREP

One day before cooking (or at least one hour before):
In a *small bowl*, mix together
- ◆ **2 tsp Baking soda**
- ◆ **1 tsp Salt**

Rub the baking soda and salt all over the skin of
- ◆ **1 pound Pork belly**

Make sure the powder is distributed evenly.

Set the pork belly on a *rack* and let it sit uncovered in the fridge for up to a day, or at least an hour before cooking.

On cooking day:

Optional:
In a *small bowl* mix and set aside to sprinkle on your chicharrones at the end (or use a readymix)
- ◆ **2 tsp Garlic powder**

Optional:
one or more of the following spices
- ◆ **1 tsp Rosemary powder**
- ◆ **1 tsp Marjoram powder**
- ◆ **To taste Cayenne powder**

Line a *plate* with *paper towels* on which to put the finished chicharrones.

Rinse the meat in cold water and pat dry.

Cut the meat into pieces about 1" long and 1/3" thick.

Place the pieces into a *wok* and add water to cover them.

Heat the wok on low. The fat will render over 2 to 4 hours, depending on the moisture content of the pork.

Turn the meat pieces every half hour or so. First, the water will look like pork stock, then it will cook off, leaving only the lard.

When only lard is left, raise the heat to high and deep fry the meat in it—about 3 to 5 minutes. Watch the meat carefully.

Using a *slotted spoon*, transfer the chicharrones to the paper-lined plate. With a couple more sheets of paper towel, gently blot them to remove excess fat.

SERVE

Toss with
   ♦ **Salt**
   ♦ The seasonings you set aside, if any

The chicharrones will remain crispy many hours.

Enjoy!

ACCENTS AND SAUCES

Accents and sauces can make a common dish come alive—like crispy herbs on roasted veggies or a balsamic vinegar sauce with its exotic tangy flavor.

Accents and sauces are often the best-kept secrets of exceptional cooks.

Crispy Herbs

A fun garnish to liven up grilled, roasted or steamed veggies, fries or meats.

MAKES 4 Cups

When to start: 30 minutes before enjoying
Hands-on time: 15 minutes
Stove time: 10 minutes

PREP

Mise en place.

Wash, *dry thoroughly* to prevent spattering, and separate the leaves from the branches of your herbs of choice, such as
 ◆ **Parsley**
 ◆ **Sage**
 ◆ **Rosemary**
 ◆ **Basil**
 ◆ **Mint**
 ◆ **Any other herbs you like**

Line a *plate* or *baking sheet* with paper towel to drain off excess fat after cooking.

COOK

Fill a *big skillet* or *heavy saucepan* with
- **1 inch Taste-free coconut oil, lard or other animal fat, or ghee**

Heat the oil on medium high until it shimmers. To test it, drop a leaf into pan. If it sizzles and floats, the oil is ready. If the leaf sinks, continue heating.

Cook the herbs in batches so they're not crowded together—about 30 seconds per batch, until crisp but not browned. They should retain some green color, looking like stained glass …

With a *slotted spoon* or *spatula*, transfer the fried herbs onto the paper-lined plate or pan and, while still hot, sprinkle generously with
- **Salt**

SERVE

Sprinkle over
- Grilled, roasted or steamed veggies
- Fries or chips
- Meats, chicken or fish

Enjoy!

Three Healing Readymixes

Who doesn't have a shelf-full of herb and spice bottles, many of them past their prime? I still have some ancient bottles in the back of my spice drawer (like those precious saffron threads that are waiting for a moment of inspiration). But unless I'm cooking something unusual (like stuffed chicken breast with coriander and cumin), I use these readymixes instead. They're made from a dozen herb and spice powders that have way-above-average health *oomph*.[58]

BUT, ALL culinary herbs and spices are highly nutritious and any one of them would be a GREAT addition to foods you cook or bring home to eat. Do feel totally free to use your favorites instead of the ones below.

Logistics (following) **and storing instructions** (at the end) **are the same for *all three* readymixes.**

MAKES ½ cup[59]

When to start:	5 minutes before enjoying
Hands-on time:	5 minutes
Stove time:	0 minutes

PREP

Mise en place.

In a **small bowl** with a **fork**, or in a **1-cup glass jar with a lid**, mix the powders, listed below.

1. PEAK PERFORMANCE READYMIX
- ◆ **2 Tb Garlic**
- ◆ **2 Tb Onion**
- ◆ **1 Tb Ginger**
- ◆ **1 Tb Turmeric**
- ◆ **1 Tb Rosemary**
- ◆ **1 Tb Oregano**
- ◆ **1 Tb Fennel seed**

---

[58] I settled on the super dozen after checking out numerous herbs and spices with medical herbalist Carol Davison and Olivier Said, owner and head teacher of a culinary school in Berkeley. Armed with our findings, we developed "Sniffle Soup," an app that offers healing blends of herbs and spices that users can customize to address over 50 common ailments. Sniffle soup also offers a few basic soup recipes in case a user doesn't have their own to use with a healing blend.

[59] The recipes for all three readymixes make 9 tablespoons of the mix, equivalent to about half a cup. The quantity fits into most recycled grocery store spice bottles.

Optional:
- **To taste Cayenne**
- **To taste Cinnamon**, preferably from Ceylon

Cayenne and cinnamon are "optional" because, while they rank at the top in health benefits, they're not for everyone. Some can't tolerate cayenne's heat, and in the West, cinnamon is typically used in sweet and fruit dishes,[60] unlike in Eastern countries,[61] where it flavors savory curries and braises.

2. MOOD READYMIX
May help alleviate depression, anxiety, and irritability.[62]

The top four
- **Cinnamon**
- **Ginger**
- **Turmeric**
- **Rosemary**

Close behind:
- **Basil**
- **Cardamom**
- **Sage**
- **Thyme**

Rosemary

Sage

Select the ones you love, in the quantities you want. You might start with one *tablespoon* of each, plus an extra tablespoon of any one—makes 9 tablespoons, the quantity that fits in a common spice bottle.

---

[60] Except in Mexico, where it flavors soups, stews, and sauces.
[61] Like India, China, and Vietnam
[62] Based on the Sniffle Soup analysis described in the first footnote at the beginning of this recipe.

3. L'IL READYMIX

Especially for a simple, familiar taste, or when you don't
have time to make a new batch of a many-ingredient
readymix.

Sumac

- **Garlic**
- **Onion**

Optional:
- **Sumac**

Sumac is a Middle Eastern herb that imparts a subtle lemony taste. It enhances both
sweet and savory food, from meat and fish to vinaigrettes, puddings, milk, and ice
cream. Used by medical people since ancient times, it is anti-inflammatory and benefits
the heart and bones.[63] I alternate sumac and cinnamon to spike a creamilk nightcap.

STORE

Transfer the readymix to a ***recycled glass spice jar*** or ***any jar with a lid*** that you can
grab easily whenever you prepare food or drink.

P.S. Fresh basil and mint, while not a readymix, comprise an important part of my
herb/spice arsenal. I harvest the leaves almost every day from the container garden on
my deck. They significantly boost the taste and health benefits of a kefir drink I have
four or five times a week, including for dinner.[64]

Extra, extra … Perhaps the most fun readymix is the one for hot chocolate. It's a combo
of cacao, cinnamon, turmeric, and salt. You'll find it in the last recipe section of this
book, "Bottoms Up."

---

[63] According to Rachael Link, MS, RD, in "Sumac Spice: The Heart-Healthy, Bone-Supporting Antioxidant" in Dr.
Axe's web site, September 1, 2018, https://draxe.com/nutrition/herbs/sumac-spice/.
[64] See recipe in "Bottoms Up" section.

Clarified Butter and Ghee

Clarified butter and ghee are premier cooking fats. They impart that wonderful butter flavor to food. Clarifying butter separates the milk solids from the fat, so that pure butter oil can be used for cooking. It imparts a butter flavor to the food without the risk of burning the milk solids, as can happen with regular butter. It is commonly used in French cooking.

To make ghee, used in Indian cooking, the milk solids released from clarifying butter are simmered in the butterfat until they caramelize. Cooking with ghee gives the food a rich, nutty flavor.

MAKES 1½ cups of butter or ghee

When to start:	25 minutes before enjoying
Hands-on time:	5 minutes
Stove time:	20 minutes

PREP

Mise en place.

CLARIFIED BUTTER

Cut into half-inch pieces and place in a ***heavy-bottomed pot***
- **1 lb Unsalted butter**

Turn heat to medium and allow butter to melt.

Gently simmer over medium-low heat until the milk solids float to the surface—about 10 to 15 minutes. The butter will bubble and foam.

Turn off the heat and remove the pan from the stove.

With a ***spoon***, remove and discard the white frothy milk solids on the surface, leaving the liquid butterfat and the white milk solids that have sunk to the bottom.

Set a ***fine-mesh strainer*** over a ***glass jar***, line the strainer with a triple layer of ***cheesecloth***, and strain the butter oil into the jar. Store at room temperature indefinitely.

VARIATION: GHEE

Ghee is clarified butter that continues to simmer after the heavy milk solids sink to the bottom. After a few minutes, the milk solids at the bottom turn light amber, and the butterfat becomes deep golden yellow. This is ghee—it smells nutty when done. Allow the ghee to slightly cool for about 3-5 minutes, then follow the clarified butter steps above—remove the froth, strain the oil, and store.

Use ghee or clarified butter to sauté or bake when you want their rich flavors to infuse the food, such as basted or fried eggs, steaks, and fish fillets.

Enjoy the richness!

Nori's No-Tomato Sauce

College nutrition teacher Nori Hudson has had a strong sensitivity to nightshades[65] and a love for spaghetti sauce since I met her over ten years ago. Undaunted, she went online and found this "no-tomato" sauce that was a hit at a nutrition book club potluck.

If you're hankering for tomato sauce but find that it causes digestive issues, joint pain, skin reddening or other signs of irritation, here's a possible alternative.

MAKES about 5 cups

When to start:	30-40 minutes before enjoying
Hands-on time:	15-20 minutes
Stove time:	20 minutes

PREP

Mise en place.

Peel and **chop** coarsely
  - **1 Onion,** to yield 3/4 cup chopped
  - **1 clove Garlic,** cut in half lengthwise (remove green stem)

Peel and cut into chunks
  - **2½ cups Carrots**

Cut into chunks
  - **1-2 Beets,** to yield 1/2 cup

beets

Steam the carrots and beets until tender, about 10 minutes, then set aside on a **plate** to cool.

With a **paring knife**, scrape the peel off the steamed beets.

Heat a **medium skillet** on medium and melt
  - **1 Tb Fat: Lard, schmaltz, or ghee**

---

[65] Nightshades are vegetables that contain substances that can irritate the digestive tracts of some people. The most common nightshades are: tomatoe (the main ingredient in spaghetti sauce), potatoes, peppers and eggplant. https://draxe.com/nightshade-vegetables

Add and brown the chopped onions and garlic (**scoop** and **spatula)**, then transfer to a plate to cool.

In a **blender or food processor**, add all prepped ingredients and blend until smooth with
- **2/3 cup Filtered water**
- **¾–1½ tsp Salt**
- **½ tsp Onion powder**
- **1/8 tsp Oregano powder**
- **1 Tb Basil leaves** (1 tsp powdered basil)
- **Lemon juice**

Optional:
Mix in cooked ground meat. (Add the quantity to the recipe yield.)

SERVE
Pour No-Tomato Sauce on any of the pancake, egg or ground meat recipes in this cookbook, on the fish fillet, Yes! Pizza, Beats Rice, or Could Be Mashed Potato. Use it as a dipping sauce for chips, fries and chicharrones.

Enjoy!

STORE
Store No-Tomato Sauce in a in the fridge. Keeps at least a couple of weeks.

Balsamic Brushing Sauce

This is the simplest sauce I have ever come across. It is just balsamic vinegar boiled down to one-half or one-third its volume. The vinegar is not the expensive aged kind, but ordinary balsamic vinegar sold in regular grocery stores. I learned how to make and use this sauce at the Green Gulch Zen Center in Mill Valley, California. I loved the veggies they served one evening and asked what the sauce was. The monk chef kindly gave me the simple technique.

Make as much as you think you can use for at least a few months. It does not need refrigeration and keeps indefinitely.

MAKES about a cup of sauce

When to start: 7 minutes before enjoying
Hands-on time: 3 minutes
Stove time: 3-5 minutes

PREP

Mise en place.

Pour into a **small saucepan** and cook over medium high heat until it has reduced to one-half or one-third its volume, 3-5 minutes
  - **2 cups Balsamic vinegar,** any ordinary supermarket variety

Taste it at one-half to decide whether to reduce it more.

SERVE

Brush on grilled, baked, or steamed vegetables; frittatas; roasted onions; poached meat; or fish.

Enjoy!

Sesame Dipping Sauce

When any meat or veggie lacks flavor, dip it or douse it with this sauce and it comes alive. I use it especially on poached chicken.

MAKES about 2/3 cup of sauce

When to start:	5 minutes before enjoying
Hands-on time:	5 minutes
Stove time:	0 minutes

PREP

Mise en place.

Into a ***small serving bowl, press, mince*** or *slice*
- **1 head (~9 cloves) Garlic**

Add and mix well with a *fork*
- **3 Tb Coconut Aminos**
- **3 Tb Sesame oil**
- **3 Tb Toasted sesame oil**

sesame seeds

SERVE

Serve as a dipping sauce with poached (or flavor-needing) meats, especially chicken, or steamed veggies.

Enjoy!

Pure Sour Cream[66]

It's really European "crème fraiche"—fermented cream, no additives of any kind. It has the rich tang of commercial sour cream without the additives that thicken it. If you've used commercial sour cream, you may find Pure Sour Cream a bit thin. But it's just as rich and tangy—and it's health-giving! You may soon prefer it.

MAKES 2 cups

When to start: 24+ hours before enjoying
Hands-on time: 5 minutes
Stove time: 0

PREP

Mise en place.

In a pint size or larger **glass jar with a lid,** mix
   ◆ **1 cup Heavy cream**
   ◆ **2 tsp   Lemon juice or white vinegar**

Add
   ◆ **¼ cup Whole milk**[67]

Screw the lid on tightly and shake well.

Replace the lid with a square of **paper towel** and secure it with either a **rubber band** or **the metal ring of your mason jar.**

Leave it at room temperature on the counter 24 hours.

Give it a stir and taste. If you want it more tangy, leave it longer.

SERVE

Put a dollop on any food to make it richer and tangier—soup, meat, steamed veggies, salad …

STORE

Lasts at least 2 weeks in the fridge.

---

[66] Based on the sour cream recipe by DIY Natural on the Bigger Bolder Baking website.
[67] Fear not—the lactose (sugar) in the milk feeds the good bacteria that create the sour cream. It disappears when the sour cream is ready.

SENSUOUS SPREADS

What better mate to legal bread than a sexy spread? They run the gamut from soft butter to bold liver pâté.

Soft Butter

Imagine having butter soft, at room temperature, any time … Well, you can have it! With a piece of pottery modeled on the centuries-old French butter crock. A "butter keeper," as it is now called, keeps butter fresh for 30 days. How? Water in the base seals the butter in the cup and keeps it from oxidizing.

I keep my butter keeper on my kitchen counter, instantly available any time I want a gob of butter on Legal Bread, Beats Rice, steamed veggies, a hardboiled egg, or a Cult cracker.

Enjoy!

Two Compound Butters: Garlic and Wild Mushroom

A compound butter is butter plus one or more ingredients. They are over-the-top nutritious and can even be healing.

A compound butter can be prepared weeks in advance and can transform an everyday dish into something extraordinary. Try it instead of a sauce. And try other ingredients like citrus peel, any fresh herb, or even anchovies or prosciutto! Just mince, mix, roll and refrigerate.

1. GARLIC BUTTER

Garlic butter is by far the most popular compound butter in the world—who hasn't savored it?

MAKES 1¼ cup

When to start: 2+ hours before enjoying
Hands-on time: 5 minutes
Stove time: 0 minutes

PREP

Mise en place.

Soften by leaving out of the fridge two or more hours depending on ambient temperature
- **1 stick (8 Tb) Butter**, preferably unsalted

Peel and *mince*
- **1 clove Fresh garlic** (or 1 tsp garlic powder)

Chop
- **2 Tb Parsley leaves**

Assemble
In a ***medium bowl***, mix all the prepped ingredients well and add
- **To taste Salt**

Take a ***sheet of wax paper***[68] and transfer the garlic butter to one edge of the sheet. Roll it into a log, twist one end shut, and secure it with a ***twist tie***, then twist the other end shut and secure it. Or put it in a ***glass or ceramic jar***.

---

[68] "Counterfold" wax paper comes in pre-cut sheets, 10-5/8" x 10-1/8". Available at amazon.com

Refrigerate the butter 12 hours or more to meld the flavors.

Use
Slice off rounds of the garlic butter to flavor cooked steaks, steamed veggies, baked chicken, poached fish, or any other food that needs more flavor.

Enjoy!

2. WILD MUSHROOM BUTTER
Wild mushrooms, with their intriguing reputation and feel of adventure, fit right into Crazy Eating—organic shitake, maitake, chaga, lion's mane, enoki, eryngii, king trumpet, chanterelles. They are neither plant nor animal; they are technically fungi, somewhere between plant and animal. Wild mushroom extracts often make up supplements to counteract serious immune ailments, but here, our interest is in their comprehensive nutrition and exotic taste. Their presence gives food a unique umami quality and satisfying mouthfeel. In powder form, wild mushrooms are a unique seasoning and they make great tea—a wild mushroom-cacao blend was a hit at a nutrition potluck I attended recently.

Wild mushroom butter can keep for several months. It is a spread (try it on Legal Bread), a flavor enhancer for steamed veggies (great in One Recipe, Many Veggies and Beats Rice), or a decadent topping for a rib eye steak, other meat, chicken, or fish.

MAKES 1¼ cup
When to start: 2+ hours before enjoying
Hands-on time: 30 minutes
Stove time: 10 minutes

PREP
Mise en place.

Soften by leaving out of the fridge one or more hours (depending on ambient temperature)
  * **1 stick (8 Tb) Butter**, preferably unsalted

Peel and *mince*
  * **1 Shallot, or the white part of 2-3 scallions, including roots**
  * **1 medium clove Garlic**

With a **mushroom or vegetable brush**, clean[69] and mince, to yield

- ½ **cup Any wild mushroom(s)** , e.g. shiitake, maitake, porcini, chanterelle, Portobello

shiitake mushrooms

(Can also use ½ oz. dried mushrooms, soaked 15 minutes in boiling water to rehydrate, or domestic button or cremini mushrooms.)

Optional:
Separate leaves and mince, to yield

- **1 tsp Fresh thyme**
- **(Or 1/8 tsp powder)**

COOK

Heat a **small, heavy skillet** on medium, and melt until it begins to foam

- **2 Tb (of the 8 Tb total) Softened butter**

Reduce the heat to medium low, add and **stir** in the minced shallot or scallion and garlic.

When the shallots/scallions are translucent and starting to caramelize, add the minced mushrooms all at once and stir, **scraping** bits that stick to the bottom of the skillet.

Optional:
Sprinkle the minced thyme over the mushrooms and cook for 1-2 minutes.

Turn off heat and allow mushrooms to cool, about 10 minutes.

In a **mixing bowl** that will also fit the mushroom mixture, add the remainder of the softened butter.

Fold the mushroom mixture into the butter until well mixed, and add

- **To taste Grinds of white pepper (black pepper ok)**

Take a sheet of **wax paper**[70] and transfer the mushroom butter to one edge of the sheet.

---

[69] Brushes to clean mushrooms (and other veggies) are available on Amazon.
[70] "Counterfold" wax paper comes in pre-cut sheets, 10-5/8"x 10-1/8". Available at Amazon.com.

Roll it into a log, twist one end shut and secure it with a ***twist tie***, then twist the other end shut **and secure it. OR put it in a glass or ceramic jar.**

Refrigerate 12 hours or more to meld the flavors.

Mushroom butter will keep in the fridge for several months. Fat is a preservative and keeps the other ingredients from going off. In the freezer, the butter will keep indefinitely.

Use
Slice off rounds of the mushroom butter to flavor cooked steaks, steamed veggies, baked chicken, poached fish, or any other food that needs more flavor. Just plop the round of on plated food and voila! you have restaurant-quality presentation and flavor.

Enjoy!

Mayo Verde

Marilyn[71] and Harvey Diamond's **"almonaise,"** in their classic *Fit for Life* cookbook, inspired this recipe... Almonaise is a **vegan spread** made with **almonds instead of eggs** and **lemon instead of vinegar**. When I finally returned to animal food in the late 1990s, I put the egg back in, kept the lemon, and **added herbs**—the "verde" that colors it a pretty light green—turning it back into *bona fide* mayonnaise.

Making your own allows you to use the best and freshest ingredients, the key to optimum health and weight loss. Once you've done it several times and have the ingredients on hand—all are common kitchen staples—making mayo **takes a mere 5 to 10 minutes.**

MAKES almost 2 cups

When to start:	10 minutes before enjoying
Hands-on time:	10 minutes
Stove time:	0 minutes

PREP

Mise en place.

Prep (***knife, cutting board***)
- **1 clove Garlic** – cut in half
- **2 stalks Scallions**[72] **o185**
- **r equivalent amount of onion** (white best) –

Cut into 1" pieces
- **1 Tb Basil leaves** or other fresh green herb, e.g., rosemary, parsley
- **1 lemon** - cut in half for squeezing

scallion

---

[71] Marilyn and Harvey divorced seven years after the publication of *Fit for Life*, a book that sold over 10 million copies, deserving a place among Wikipedia's Best Selling Books in History. A year later, Marilyn married Donald Schnell, a doctor of clinical hypnotherapy, and together they wrote *Young for Life*, their advice on longevity, published in 2013.

[72] Include the roots of the scallions, which are especially nutritious.

"COOK"

Put in a *food processor* or *blender*
- ◆ **About 2 Tb Lemon juice**

The prepped herbs
- ◆ **2 tsp Dijon-type mustard**
- ◆ **¼ tsp Salt**

Process until the herbs almost dissolve

Add
- ◆ **1 Egg**
- ◆ **1 Egg yolk**[73]

Blend about 15 seconds

Pour into a *measuring cup*
- ◆ **1 cup Virgin olive oil**

Turn the machine back on and slowly pour the oil in a thin stream.

With a clean finger, test the texture and taste of the mayo. If too thick, add drops of water. If too thin, add a little oil. If lacking in taste, add salt or mustard.

STORE

Store in a *glass jar* in the fridge. Usually keeps 3 to 6 weeks if refrigerated immediately after each use.

VARIATIONS:
1. **Garlic aioli:** Roast 1 head of garlic, mash into a paste and add to the mayo.
2. **Tartar sauce:** Mince sugar-free pickles (or cucumber) and hardboiled egg, and mix into the mayo.
3. **Blue cheese sauce:** Add sour cream or coconut cream and crumbled blue cheese or Roquefort to taste.

Enjoy!

---

[73] Save the white for future use. I usually add it to basted or zucchini-bottom eggs.

Poly Pesto

For years I bought organic pesto from a young French man at the North Berkeley farmers market. Then I moved … Now I make my own. I never realized how easy, quick and versatile it is. I use it with so many dishes … But you do need a food processor.

MAKES about 1½ cup

When to start: If low-roasted or soaked g are available, 20 minutes before using
If nuts need to be treated, 1 hr. 15 min. to a day before using
Hands-on time: 15-20 minutes
Stove time: If treated nuts are available, 0 minutes

PREP

Mise en place.

Peel, remove the green stem, and set aside
- **2 cloves Garlic**

Separate the leaves and set aside
- **2 *cup*s Herb or herb combo you like:**
Basil is the traditional herb for pesto
Parsley is always available
Arugula is exotic and adds a pungent note

Experiment with different herbs. All herbs give awesome nutrition, so let your palate be the judge.

Cut into chunks or **grate** and add to **a food processor**[74]
- **½ cup Parmesan, pecorino or other dry cheese**

---

[74] See graters in the section on kitchen tools at the end of this cookbook.

COOK

Add to the processor
- **¼ cup Treated[75] walnuts, pecans, or pine nuts[76]**

Pulse until nuts and cheese are crumbly.

- Add the garlic and herbs, and pulse to combine.

Turn the processor on and slowly pour in a thin stream
- **½ cup Olive oil**

Taste the pesto and add salt if needed.

Scrape down the sides of the processor and blend just a few more seconds.

Transfer to a *glass or ceramic container with cover*, or use immediately.

SERVE

Pesto transforms any food you put it on or mix it with—especially chicken or vegetables. It's a great spread on zucchini or radish slices or chips. And spreading it on pizza crust instead of the usual tomato sauce makes the pizza special.

Enjoy!

STORE

Refrigerate Poly Pesto in a glass jar in the fridge. It lasts about 2 weeks—if it's not devoured sooner.

---

[75] Low-roasted or soaked to remove anti-nutrients nuts naturally contain. **Low roasting**: Bake at 225° F 30-60 minutes. The nuts are done when they turn golden brown and you can smell their fragrance. Soaking: Put nuts in a glass jar and fill with double the amount of water. Soak for about 18 hours. The antinutrients in the nuts go into the water. Change the water several times during soaking—when it gets very cloudy. After soaking, dry the nuts either in a dehydrator or in an oven up to 118° F.

[76] Pine nuts are the traditional pesto ingredient, but they're relatively expensive and the other nuts work as well. The Berkeley farmers market pesto was made with walnuts.

Cream Cheese

Cream cheese is not fattening. The milk sugar is strained out, leaving the fat that forms the curds we eat. The procedure described here is based on chef Gemma Stafford's instructions on her website, Bigger Bolder Baking.[77]

MAKES about 1 lb.

When to start: 40 minutes before enjoying
Hands-on time: 25 minutes
Cooking time: 15 minutes

PREP

Mise en place.

Juice
  ♦ **4-5 Lemons**, to yield ½ cup juice
(Can also use lime juice or white vinegar.)

In a **4-quart saucepan,** heat on medium high, stirring constantly until it gets to a rolling simmer
  ♦ **2 qt + 1 cup Milk**

Reduce the heat to medium and add the lemon juice one **tablespoon** at a time, in 1-minute intervals while stirring.

lemon

Cook

until the mixture curdles and has separated completely—just a few minutes. Then remove from heat. There will be a green liquid on the bottom and thick curds on top.

Put a *sieve* over a **large bowl,** lay in a double layer of **cheesecloth,** and pour the curd mixture into the sieve, letting it strain and cool, about 15 minutes.

Transfer the curds to a **food processor** and process until totally smooth and creamy, about 3-4 minutes or longer.

Towards the end of processing, add
  ♦ **½ tsp (to taste) Salt**

---

[77] https://www.biggerbolderbaking.com/how-to-make-cream-cheese/

Optional:
- **Powdered herbs and spices you like**, e.g. garlic, onion, basil, cinnamon

Taste and adjust …

Transfer the cheese to one side of a **counterfold wax paper sheet**[78] and roll to form a log, **or** put it in **a glass or ceramic jar or serving dish**.

Enjoy!

P.S. This cream cheese is the main ingredient in Crazy Cheesecake (recipe coming up).

STORE

If you rolled the cream cheese in wax paper, secure it at both ends with **twist ties** and put the log in a **plastic bag** to help prevent drying out.

Store in the fridge, where it can last up to 2 weeks, or freeze it.

---

[78] Counterfold wax paper is pre-cut 10" x 10 ¾," a wonderful time saver.

Laura's Liver Pâté

Before I tried this pâté at a nutrition club potluck meeting, I had never thought to make it myself. I'd buy it from gourmet grocers or European delis. Laura's liver pâté changed that ... From memory, she told us how she made it that morning.

MAKES 6 to 8 servings

When to start: 1 hr. 45 min. before enjoying
Hands-on time: 10 minutes
Stove time: 25 minutes
Chill time: 1 hour

PREP

Thinly *slice* and add to a ***medium saucepan***
- **1 Onion**

In a ***food processor***, mince
- **1 Onion** (in addition to the sliced onion)
- **2 cloves Garlic**

Rinse, cut into chunks and add to the saucepan
- **1 lb Liver—chicken, beef, or pork**

COOK

Bring to boil the liver and sliced onion with
- **3 cups Water**

Reduce heat to low and simmer ~20 mins.

Drain and put the liver and onions in the food processor, along with
- **¾ cup Butter**
- **¼ tsp Salt**
- **¼ tsp Pepper**
- **1/8 tsp Mace**

Optional: **3 Tb Sherry or cognac**

Process to combine, then form the mixture into a mound, or pack it into a mason jar, and chill 1 hour. ***Enjoy!***

STORE

Put into a ***mason jar***, add a thin layer of pork/chicken/duck fat or butter or olive oil on top, and close the jar tightly. Lasts about a week in the fridge or two months in the freezer.

OH SO SWEET

The basic Crazy Eating formula for sweet:
lots of *qualified* butter, heavy cream, or coconut
oil + a few drops of monk fruit extract.

The recipes also use other qualified fats:
sour cream or crème fraiche, cream cheese,
cocoa butter, and egg yolks—and vanilla extract
for extra sweetening ...

Really Chocolate

She looked suspiciously at the jagged piece of chocolate I offered. She smelled it, then warily put it in her mouth. I wish I had had a camera to capture the big smile and the happy twinkle in her eyes. "Do you have more?" she asked, and eagerly grabbed two more big pieces … I sighed with relief. My friend Lulu is a lifelong chocolate aficionado and turns her nose up at the 100%-cacao, sugar-free chocolate that's come on the scene recently. Her opinion represents lots of people who like traditional European chocolate.

Then she asked, "Is it really healthy? Can I eat all I want without worrying?" I assured her that there was not a shadow of sugar in the chocolate, and that she was getting a ton of antioxidants that come in pure chocolate, plus more than 80 natural minerals from the Himalayan salt. She beamed and took two more pieces.

chocolate

The secret is in the cacao butter—the part of the cacao bean that gives chocolate its melt-in-your-mouth quality.

The second secret is the monk fruit extract—a healthy sweetener that has none of the bitter aftertaste of stevia.

MAKES about 6 full-size chocolate bars[79]

VARIATION 1: CHOCOLATE BARS _WITHOUT_ NUTS
When to start: 45 min. to 1 hr. 15 min. before enjoying
Hands-on time: 7 minutes
Stove time: 5 minutes
Freezer / fridge time: 30 / 60 minutes

VARIATION 2: CHOCOLATE BARS _WITH_ NUTS
When to start: 1-2 hours before enjoying
Hands-on time: 10 minutes
Stove time: 20-45 minutes
Freezer / fridge time: 30 / 60 minutes

PREP

Mise en place.

---

[79] Based on averaging the full sizes of 5 brands: The Good Chocolate, MI Chocolate, Green & Black's, Bulletproof and Hershey. Green & Black's and The Good Chocolate were the largest at 17.6 and 17 square inches, respectively; Hershey's and Bulletproof the smallest at 11.4 and 12.2 square inches, respectively.

<u>*Only for NUTS:*</u> Low-roast[80] walnuts, hazelnuts, almonds, or other nuts:
Preheat oven to 225° F.

On a **cutting board**, with a **heavy meat pounder**, break into pieces. A few light hits can break the nuts up enough.

- ¾ to 1 cup Nuts

On a **baking sheet**, spread the nut pieces in a single layer and roast until fragrant and slightly golden, 15-40 minutes.[81]

Line **another baking sheet (at least 9" x 12")** with **parchment paper**, OR, position your **chocolate molds** for filling.

COOK

Over medium heat, melt in a double boiler, or in a **glass mixing bowl set in a small saucepan** with 1 inch of water,
- **1 cup Cacao/cocoa butter**[82]

Remove cacao butter from heat and **whisk** in to combine
- **1/4 tsp Monk fruit extract**

When the mixture is completely fluid with no separation, add and thoroughly combine
- **1 cup Unsweetened cacao/cocoa powder**
- **1 tsp Vanilla extract**

Taste and adjust sweetness if needed.

Pour the chocolate into the lined baking sheet or molds. Top with
- **1 tsp Salt**
- The low-roasted nuts if using

Set in freezer or refrigerator to harden, 30 minutes to 1 hour.

Once completely solid, break or cut into pieces/bars, or remove from molds. **Enjoy!**

STORE

Store the leftover chocolate pieces in an **airtight container** in the refrigerator for 2-3 weeks, or in a **freezer bag** in the freezer 1-2 months.

---

[80] Low-roasting raw nuts (preferably organic) at 225° F for about 30 minutes to an hour reduces anti-nutrients naturally found in nuts.

[81] The time range is big due to differences in nut texture and individual oven heat.

[82] If you can't find cocoa butter, try coconut oil—cup for cup.

Kris's Chocolate Coconut Crunch

Seven clinical nutritionists gobbled up this luncheon dessert, everyone going for seconds without a second thought. Yes, chocolate without the usual sugar and milk additives is healthy, brimming with antioxidants and other nutrients. So is coconut.

This dessert was created by Kris Homme, author of many professional journal articles on mercury poisoning.[83] Kris needs to eat healthy religiously to prevent further brain degeneration from mercury poisoning. Happily for us, she makes sure that the food she eats (and brings to our potlucks) is always a pleasure. What better ingredients than chocolate and coconut!

coconut

MAKES about 25 two-inch-square pieces

When to start: At least 1 hr. 15-20 min. before enjoying
Hands-on time: 10 minutes
Stove time: 8-10 minutes
Fridge time: 1+ hours

PREP

Mise en place.

In a **small pan** over medium low heat, melt
* **1 cup Coconut oil**
(If your ambient temperature is above 76º F, your coconut oil may already be melted.)

In a **double boiler** over medium heat (or in a **glass mixing bowl set in a small saucepan** with 1 inch of water), melt
* **2 oz Unsweetened chocolate**

[83] For example, Sarah Russell and Kristen Homme, "Mercury, the quintessential anti-nutrient," *Townsend Letter,* January 2017, www.townsendletter.com/Jan2017/mercury0117.html

Line a **baking pan (about 9" x 12" or bigger)** with **parchment paper**.

Add to the pan in order:

- **1 cup Dried coconut flakes or chips**
- The melted Coconut oil
- The melted Chocolate
- **1 tsp Salt**

Refrigerate an hour or more. Cut into pieces and serve.

Enjoy!

Sweet Cream Ice Cream

You'll need an ice cream maker, but no worries if you don't have one. You'll find them at a local kitchen store or online at a wide price range—from under $30 to over $200.

SERVES 4-8

When to start: At least 1 hr. 10 min. before enjoying
Hands-on time: 8-10 minutes
Stove time: 0 minutes
Freezer time: 1+ hours

PREP

Mise en place.

Into a **medium bowl,** whisk together
- **2¼ cups + 2 Tb Heavy cream**
- **½ cup + 2 Tb Water**
- **2 tsp Monk fruit extract**
- **1/8 tsp Salt**
- **1 Tb Vanilla extract**

Optional: If <u>not</u> on a fat-burning plan, cut into small pieces and add to bowl
- **2 cups Berries or low-roasted nuts and seeds, chocolate, coconut chips, or whatever you like** … but let it be healthy.

Pour the mix into the **ice cream maker** and churn according to manufacturer's instructions.

Transfer the ice cream to an **airtight container** and freeze.

Enjoy!

Banana Only Ice Cream

IMPORTANT: If you hold metabolic positions 3, 4 or 5,[84] make this only for Anything Goes Day[85] or if you are *not* watching your waistline. This recipe is here because it's so much healthier than regular ice cream—which contains sugar and pasteurized milk.

I recently made this recipe with my friend Floreni. As she was puréeing the frozen banana, she asked if we had forgotten the sugar and milk … All we added to the banana after puréeing were a couple of handfuls of chopped macadamia nuts and pecans—because I love crunchy nuts in ice cream.

This recipe is for peeps who are transitioning from a diet with sugar and milk to one without, as well as for those who are in the "leisurely" metabolic positions 1 or 2.

SERVES 2

When to start: At least 1-2 hrs. 15-20 mins. before enjoying (shorter time for soft-serve texture)

Hands-on time: About 15 minutes

Stove time: 0 minutes

Freezer time: 1-2+ hours

PREP

Mise en place.

Peel, wrap individually in **wax paper,** and freeze
  ◆ **2 bananas**

Cut the frozen bananas into 1-inch pieces and add to **food processor or blender.**

Optional:
For creamier texture, add
  ◆ **¼ cup Coconut milk**

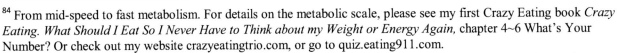

banana

---

[84] From mid-speed to fast metabolism. For details on the metabolic scale, please see my first Crazy Eating book *Crazy Eating. What Should I Eat So I Never Have to Think about my Weight or Energy Again,* chapter 4~6 What's Your Number? Or check out my website crazyeatingtrio.com, or go to quiz.eating911.com.

[85] Anything Goes Day is described in the second Crazy Eating book: *Crazy Eating in the Land of Foodlike Substances,* chapter 2~17 Anything Goes Day.

For easier scooping out when frozen,
Add

* **1 Tb Vodka**

If using, cut into small pieces and set aside to add after processing
* **Nuts**
* **Fruit**

Process or blend until smooth like ice cream, occasionally scraping down the sides of the machine with a ***rubber spatula***—3-5 minutes.

Optional:
Fold in one or more:
* **Nuts and/or fruit pieces**
* **Nut butter**
* **Cacao nibs**
* **Spices**

pecans

SERVE/STORE

For soft-serve, scoop the ice cream directly into serving dishes.

Otherwise, put it into an ***airtight, freezer-safe container*** and freeze at least one hour.

Enjoy!

Cheesecake Celebration[86]

Maybe it's your birthday, someone important's birthday, a wedding, or some very special day. It's time for cake!

If you use clean, well-sourced, intelligent ingredients in your cake, it will not be fattening. Instead, it can be energizing and even health-giving! You might think, well, almond flour has carbs … Yes, but the quantity is negligible—one net carb gram per slice. Regular cheesecake has a whopping 20 net carb grams per slice. Plus, almond flour is clean, real, and whole, not stripped or contaminated with toxicants.

If you want to hold out for zero carbs, just don't eat the crust. It's that thin golden brown bottom that makes it look like a traditional cheesecake and gives it a lovely nutty accent. But it's not necessary. If you omit it, you'll save significant kitchen time.

MAKES a 7 to 9-inch cheesecake with crust

When to start:	The day before enjoying
Hands-on time:	20 minutes
Stove time:	1-2 hours 10 minutes
Cooling time:	60 minutes on kitchen counter
Fridge time:	Overnight

PREP

Mise en place.

THE CRUST
Preheat oven to 350° F (175° C).

Butter a *7-inch or 9-inch springform pan*, OR line the base with *parchment paper*.

In a *small saucepan*, soften
- **2 oz. Butter**

Optional:
To get a lovely toffee flavor, heat the butter until it smells nutty.[87]

---

[86] Based on Anne Aobadia's recipe for "keto cheesecake with blueberries" on Dietdoctor.com.
https://www.dietdoctor.com/recipes/low-carb-cheesecake
[87] For more detailed instructions, check out how to make ghee in the recipe Clarified Butter and Ghee in the section "Sensuous Spreads".

Remove the butter from the heat and add to the pan
- **1 ¼ cups Almond flour**
- **10 drops Monk fruit extract**
- **½ tsp Vanilla extract**

Combine all into a dough and press it into the base of the springform pan.

Bake 8 minutes, until the crust turns light golden.

Take out of the oven and allow to cool.

THE FILLING
Raise the oven heat to 400º F (200º C).

Into a *small bowl* add
- **2 Eggs**
- **1 Egg yolk**

With a *lemon zester or vegetable peeler*, zest and add to the eggs
- **1 tsp Lemon zest** (from 1 lemon)

In a *large bowl*, mix together
- **1 lb Cream cheese** (see recipe in Sensuous Spreads)
- **½ cup Heavy cream or crème fraiche**
- **½ tsp Vanilla extract**
- The eggs, egg yolk and lemon zest

Pour the mixture into the springform pan over the crust and bake 15 minutes.

Lower the heat to 230º F (110º C) and bake another 45-60 minutes.

Turn off the heat and let the cake cool in the oven.

When the cake has cooled completely (about one hour), refrigerate overnight.

SERVE

Optional:
- *Cut* up fresh berries for garnish. Raspberries, blackberries and strawberries have the lowest carb percentage (5-6%). Blueberries have double, at 12%. But the pièce de résistance is the cheesecake.

Enjoy! And feel free to go for a second slice!

Edi's Persimmon Parfait

Edi Pfeiffer, a classic homeopath and dear friend, created this nondairy parfait from a recipe she happened upon online. Edi's creation is a delight to look at as well as to eat!

These are smaller than Edi's parfaits, to lower the net carbs from those deliciously ripe persimmons. If you're not watching your carbs—i.e., your waistline—go for an additional layer each of chia cream and persimmon.

persimmon

SERVES 6

When to start: 8 hrs. 15 min., or the day before enjoying
Hands-on time: 15 minutes
Stove time: 0 minutes

THE CHIA PUDDING[88]

PREP

Mise en place.

Whisk together in an ***airtight quart container***
- ♦ **2 cups Coconut milk**
- ♦ **½ cup Chia seeds**
- ♦ **1 ½ tsp Vanilla extract (or the seeds of 1 vanilla bean pod**[89]**)**
- ♦ **½ tsp Ground cinnamon**
- ♦ **¼ tsp Ground cardamom**

Refrigerate overnight or at least 8 hours.

---

[88] Did you know that chia pudding eaten at bedtime is a natural remedy for constipation? Put 2 tablespoons seeds in ½ cup water, wait about half an hour for it to gel, then eat. In the morning you may be pleasantly surprised... To address constipation you can make this simple version all by itself.
[89] To use a vanilla bean pod, take a paring knife and split the pod down its length. Scrape out the seeds and use immediately for best flavor.

THE PERSIMMON CREAM – Make *after* refrigerating the pudding

PREP

Mise en place.

Wash and de-stem
- **5 Very ripe persimmons**

In a *food processor or blender*, process until smooth
- The de-stemmed persimmons
- **¼ tsp Ground cinnamon**

SERVE

Set out *6 serving glasses—champagne glasses are great.*

In each glass, create 4 layers, alternating 1 rounded Tb pudding, then 1 Tb persimmon cream.

Don't worry about perfect presentation. The gorgeous persimmon color covers up any inadvertent sloppiness!

Enjoy!

Cozy Custard—aka Vanilla Pudding

Custard was my ultimate comfort food growing up. I loved licking the wooden stirring spoon and scraping—right into my mouth—the warm golden goo that stuck to the sides of the pot when it was done. But most of all, I loved eating the custard. Way back then, in the Philippines, milk was *not* pasteurized and eggs were *all* pasture-raised from chickens that had grown up in our garden. Except for the sugar, it was a health food.

All I've done to update my mom's recipe is replace sugar with Monk fruit extract and milk with creamilk.

SERVES 4

When to start:	About 2 ½ hours before enjoying
Hands-on time:	6 minutes
Stove time:	20-25 minutes
Cooling time:	1 hour
Chilling time:	1 hour

PREP

Mise en place.

Put in a **medium bowl**
- **3 Egg yolks**, reserving the whites for a future recipe, e.g., cheesecake

COOK

In a **small saucepan**, heat on medium low to medium, just until small bubbles form around the sides of the pan (do not boil), about 5 minutes
- **1 cup Heavy cream**
- **1 cup Water**
- **1 tsp Vanilla extract** (or the seeds of ½ vanilla bean pod)

Add to the egg yolks and **whisk** until frothy
- **10 drops Monk fruit extract**
- **Pinch Salt**

Stir in
- Half of the hot creamilk[90]

Then pour the mixture into the saucepan with the remaining creamilk.

---

[90] Creamilk is a mix of heavy cream and water.

Turn the heat to low or medium low— keep the heat low enough so you don't get scrambled eggs. Cook the custard 15-20 minutes, stirring frequently with *a wooden spoon*. Towards the end, stir continuously.

Remove the saucepan from the heat and continue stirring another minute or so, to release some heat.

Leave the custard on the counter to cool.

SERVE
Serve at room temp or chill in fridge before serving.

For an added gob of pleasure, *whip* some cream and swirl it on top, then dust with nutmeg.

Enjoy!

Berries (or Peaches[91]) and Cream

Strawberries-and-cream was my stepfather's favorite dessert when I was growing up. This recipe replaces the sugar without compromising on sweetness and increases the quality of the ingredients—from conventional to organic berries and from pasteurized to raw cream. I always feel a bit nostalgic when I make it ...

If you're sensitive to dairy, do skip this recipe and move on to the next, which replaces cream with coconut kefir.

Happily, strawberries happen to be among the berries lowest in net carbs, along with raspberries and blackberries. If you're not on a strict fat-burning plan, blueberries are ok, or even peaches, both in the mid-range for net carbs.[92]

strawberry

MAKES 4 servings

When to start:	10 min. to 1 hr. 10 minutes before enjoying
Hands on time:	10 minutes
Optional chilling time:	30 minutes to an hour

PREP

Mise en place.

Wash, drain, and ***de-stem***
- **2 cups Berries**: for strict fat-burning, use strawberries, blackberries, or raspberries

ASSEMBLE

In a ***large bowl***, mash with a ***potato masher*** or ***fork***
- ½ cup (not all) **Berries**
- **0-5 drops Monk fruit extract**
- Add the rest of the berries and mix together.

---

[91] Peaches are ok if you're not on a strict fat-burning plan. They are in the mid range of net carb percentages in fruits, as shown in the Nitty Gritty "Net Carbs in Fruits" at the end of the book.
[92] *Ibid.*

In a **small bowl,** mix

- ¼ cup **Sour cream or crème fraiche** (next recipe is nondairy)
- ¾ cup **Heavy cream**
- **0-5 drops Monk fruit extract**

Pour cream over the berries.

SERVE

Serve as-is or chill.

Enjoy!

heavy cream

Coconut Kefir Berries

Coconut kefir sauce is a great alternative to cream on fruit. It takes only a few minutes of hands-on time and contributes much to digestive health.

Clinical nutritionist Tamar Cohen[93] brought this sauce to a book club potluck. She used dairy kefir grains to ferment coconut milk, knowing that the voracious bacteria weren't picky, serving it with blueberries because no one was watching their waistline. Strawberries, blackberries, or raspberries, which are significantly lower in net carbs, are a better choice on a fat-burning plan.[94]

SERVES 4–6

When to start: About a week before enjoying
Hands-on time: 5 minutes
Stove time: 0 minutes

PREP

Mise en place.

Pour into a *glass or ceramic container*
   ◆ **1 quart Coconut milk**

Add
   ◆ **2 Tb Milk-kefir grains**[95]

Cover the jar with a *paper towel or cheesecloth* secured with a *rubber band, string, or metal jar-cover ring* and let it sit on your kitchen counter about a week.

Taste for doneness. Then, stir gently and strain the kefir through a *non-metal* colander into a bowl. Transfer the kefir to a glass bottle[96] until ready to use.

Select your fruit: strawberries, blackberries or raspberries—any one or all three.

SERVE

Prepare the berries and put them into *a serving bowl or individual dessert dishes*, leaving room for the sauce. Pour the coconut kefir sauce generously over the berries.

Enjoy for dessert or breakfast!

---

[93] Tamar Cohen, tamar@triholisticnutrition.com, 510-919-8725
[94] See Nitty Gritty "Carbs in Fruit" at the end of the book.
[95] Available from kefirlady.com, who mails authentic kefir grains to customers all over the United States.
[96] You can also scoop out the grains and transfer the grains to a new jar, keeping the kefir in the original soaking jar.

Golden Door Stuffed Date

I'll always remember being greeted by a young woman offering me a weird-looking dark brown blob on an exquisite plate. I had just stepped through the golden door at the entrance of the original Golden Door in Southern California,[97] a now globally famous and uber expensive health spa. Skeptically, I bit into the strange treat and was astonished at its subtle yet intense sweetness, combined with a fun crunch. There was no platter for seconds—just one divine pecan-stuffed date.

The Golden Door date was at room temperature and the pecan was raw. Served that way, it would take less than a minute to prepare two stuffed dates. At home, we first remove anti-nutrients from the nuts and add a dollop of whipped raw cream or coconut kefir sauce to smooth everything out ...

Don't be tempted to have seconds. Dates are normally a "don't" in Crazy Eating, but once in a while for a special occasion, treat yourself and a loved one to the sweet that welcomes new guests to a world-class health spa.

SERVES 2

When to start: If you *don't* have pre-treated nuts, 1 hour to 2 days before enjoying
If you *have* pre-treated nuts, 10 minutes before enjoying
Hands on time: 5-10 minutes
Stove time: 5-8 minutes

PREP

Mise en place.

---

[97] At its original location in Escondido, a small town near San Diego, California, when the cost of a week there was $900, in 1980 U.S. dollars.

THE NUTS

If you don't have a Crazy Eating nut stash prepared, remove the nuts' natural anti-nutrients by either low-roasting or soaking them. Low roasting is faster and yields crunchier nuts; soaking (then drying) removes more anti-nutrients. The quantity in this recipe will yield many more nuts than you need, but you'll have a stash that will eliminate this step the next time you make this exotic treat.

Low-Roast

Turn oven on to 225° F.

Add to a **baking pan** in a single layer
- **Pecans or your choice of nut** (more than you need to have some left over)

Roast 30-60 minutes. They're done when golden brown, fragrant and crunchy.

Use immediately or cool to room temperature and store in a **glass jar**.

Soak: To a **quart glass jar** add
- **1 cup Pecans or other nut of choice**
- 3 cups Water

Leave on counter to soak for at least 18 hours, replacing the water several times or whenever it gets cloudy.

Drain the nuts and dry them in a dehydrator or oven at about 120° F.

Use immediately or cool to room temperature and store in a clean, dry **glass jar**.

THE DATES

Heat oven to 275° F.

Cut in half and remove the seed from
- **2 Medjool dates**

Warm the dates in the oven about 5 minutes.

Optional:
- **The Cream Topping.** Cream contributes a sensuous, velvety quality to each bite. Select either dairy or coconut.

Dairy Cream tones down the date's intense sweetness. Whip with a ***hand mixer, immersion blender, whisk or fork***

- ¼ cup Heavy cream, preferably raw[98]

Coconut Cream intensifies the date's sweetness. Stir the coconut cream to make sure the coconut oil is mixed in with the coconut mass. If the coconut cream has solidified, warm it in a 225° F oven to soften.

- ¼ cup Coconut cream[99]

SERVE

Put one date open-faced on each serving plate.

Place nuts on top of each date—just enough to cover the date.

Optional:
Top with a dollop of **whipped** dairy or coconut cream. ***Enjoy!***

---

[98] Raw cream can be refrigerated indefinitely. It simply becomes sour, then it can be used as sour cream or crème fraiche.

[99] Tropical Traditions, Nutiva, or other organic product. Coconut cream can be kept on your counter; it doesn't go bad. I have a small jar that I often go to after a good dinner. It solidifies at room temperature, so I use a small knife to cut a piece that includes both the oil on top and the sweet coconut mass underneath. The piece goes from jar to mouth …

BOTTOMS UP!

There's an array of delicious drink recipes coming up, but first I must rant about an ingredient in most of them—water, the mother of drinks.

BEWARE TAP WATER!

Unfiltered, tap water harbors added chemicals to disinfect the now traces of formaldehyde). name of health, when it is industry is getting rid of contain lead, linked to a proficiency scores. The 1,000 water systems pipes.

pesticides from agricultural runoff and water (like chlorine and ammonia, and Many cities also add fluoride in the actually a waste product the aluminum profitably.[100] Sometimes aging water pipes dramatic drop in children's reading and mental Environmental Working Group reports that over nationwide have elevated lead levels from old

But the scariest is the presence of pharmaceuticals. I don't need anxiety medications, anticonvulsants, or betablockers; not even baby aspirin. A nationally funded study in Ontario, Canada found "quantifiable pharmaceuticals" in the tap water of 14 communities, some with 31 different pharmaceuticals[101] …

While treatment plants do a good job of filtering out normal-size waste molecules (with the use of chemicals, of course), *"nanomedicines"* flow right through the treatments and into our tap water. Nanomedicines are microscopic packets of pharmaceuticals targeted at specific body tissues, like cancer tumors. Because they are unimaginably tiny, they are not caught in water treatment traps.[102]

Imagine the handfuls of prescription pills people take every day … and have taken over several decades … Pills people flush down the toilet … The cumulative effect is frightening.

Bottled water, then? Yes and no. If the bottles are glass, yes. If plastic, NO! We don't know how long bottles sit in a hot warehouse before landing in a grocery store. Over time, microscopic plastic particles leach into the water, according to researchers who analyzed leading international brands of plastic-bottled water, including those in the U.S., Germany, China, India, Mexico, Brazil, and Indonesia. And don't be fooled by "BPA[103]-free."

---

[100] Joseph Mercola, Fluoride: Poison On Tap, October 14, 2017, https://articles.mercola.com/archive/2017/10/14/fluoride-poison-on-tap-documentary.aspx.

[101] Laurie Chan, et al. First Nations Food, Nutrition & Environmental Study: Results from Ontario 2011–2012. http://www.fnfnes.ca/docs/FNFNES_Ontario_Regional_Report_2014_final.pdf

[102] Leigh Boerner, "The Complicated Question of Drugs in the Water," PBS SoCal, May 14, 2014. https://www.pbs.org/wgbh/nova/article/pharmaceuticals-in-the-water/

[103] BPA is a chemical used in the manufacture of plastic. The U.S. FDA (Food and Drug Administration) banned it from baby bottles and sippy cups in 2012, triggering a plethora of plastic products labelled BPA-free.

The chemicals that replace BPA are, sadly, as harmful if not more. For example, BPS "disrupts hormones, makes you fat, and alters your brain," declares Dr. Fred Pescatore in his newsletter.[104]

Too many plastic bottles end up as floating debris in the ocean, eaten by unsuspecting fish. Ecologists have found plastic in the intestines of a quarter of the fish and a third of shellfish sold in the United States and Indonesia. Beth Terry's book on getting rid of plastic in her life reports this unappetizing tidbit and many other horrific and little-known facts about omni-present plastic.[105]

So, what water is a girl or boy to drink?

I drink reverse-osmosis-filtered water that is re-mineralized after it has been purified. Reverse osmosis removes toxicants like fluoride, chlorine, ammonia, and microscopic pharmaceuticals, but it can also remove minerals we need for health, like magnesium and potassium. That is why re-mineralization is important.

Water Temperature: Water at or a bit higher than body temperature conserves the body's energy—the body doesn't have to heat it up, like it does when you drink ice-cold water.

Sometimes you'll see weight-loss suggestions to drink cold water. Why? Because common weight loss strategies rely on using up or restricting energy (in the form of calories). However, we don't want to use up the precious energy we need to work, play, and live. We want to drop weight by burning *fat*, which *creates* energy. And the quickest way to burn fat is to reduce or eliminate carbohydrates and toxic food.

A U.S. government-funded study reports that the ideal temperature for drinking hot beverages is 136° F. Serendipitously, the owners of Driftaway Coffee in Brooklyn, New York, report that their customers enjoy coffee the most at 120–140° F. That feels right—normal body temperature is 96.8° F and boiling happens at 212° F …

In addition to the benefits of drinking water in general, hot water:
- Helps digestion—it breaks food down faster and supports bowel movements.
- Expands blood vessels, which improves circulation and helps muscles relax.
- Increases metabolism during the hour after consumption.

AND it is such a pleasure to sit quietly first thing in the morning with a cup of hot water to wake me up gently; then, last thing at night to relax slowly.

Ahhhhh.

---

[104] *Logical Alternatives*, Volume 6, Issue 8, August 2016.
[105] Beth Terry, *Plastic Free: How I Kicked the Plastic Habit and How You Can Too,* New York: Sky Horse Publishing, 2015.

Real-Cream Soda

Trying to get off sodas? ...

MAKES about 14 ounces

When to start: 3 minutes before enjoying
Hands-on time: 3 minutes
Stove time: 0 minutes

PREP

Mise en place.

In a ***shaker or pint sized glass jar***, mix
- ½ cup Kombucha—any flavor you enjoy
- 1 cup Mineral or sparkling water
- 2-4 Tb Heavy cream

Taste and adjust if necessary.

Enjoy!

Creamilk

Love milk but don't want its (natural) sugar?

A diabetic colleague switched to creamilk when she got a Type 2 diabetes diagnosis ... A client on my fat-burning program, who was a milk addict, confessed that at first she missed her nightly glass of regular milk, but soon forgot about it and happily drank her glass of creamilk before bed.

Last month I made it for my niece Annie, who loves to cook. She smiled, then asked: "Ok to add vanilla and a sprinkle of cinnamon?" That subtly sweeter variation has become a frequent dessert or nightcap for me, often with just cinnamon.

SERVES the number you choose

When to start: 3 minutes before enjoying
Hands-on time: 3 minutes
Stove time: 0 minutes

PREP

Mise en place.

In a **glass or pitcher**, mix
  ◆ **1 part Heavy cream**
  ◆ **2 parts Water**

Mix, taste, and adjust if necessary. If too thick, add water. If too thin, add cream.

Optional:
For a sweeter taste and added flavor, add
  ◆ **1/8-1/4 tsp Vanilla extract**

For a spike in flavor and attractiveness, sprinkle on top
  ◆ **1/8 tsp Cinnamon powder**—Ceylon cinnamon[106] if possible

Enjoy!

---

[106] Ceylon cinnamon does not contain coumarin, a substance in cassia and Vietnamese/Saigon cinnamon that acts as a blood thinner. The cassia plant, from the pea family, is the source of most cinnamon sold in the United States. Ceylon cinnamon, from the cinnamon tree, is known as the "true" cinnamon and is available in herb stores and many supermarkets.

Vic's Veggie Juice

Vic Link, a "sugar rehab coach" who practices in Petaluma, California, calls this recipe her "Hydrate-Me Quik" drink. It floated into her head when she was fiercely thirsty one day "out in the field" working.

Some years ago, Vic and I organized and directed several juice fasts, each attended by some 30 people eager to clean out their bodies in a secluded retreat setting while learning about nutrition. Vic created all the juice formulas and supervised their making. Participants knew the fruit juices would be sweet treats, but were always surprised that they actually enjoyed the *veggie* juices too!

P.S. The fruit juices were all diluted with water to prevent overloading with fruit sugar.

MAKES about 6 cups

When to start:	5–10 minutes before enjoying
Hands-on time:	5–10 minutes
Stove time:	0 minutes

PREP

Mise en place.

Peel
- ◆ **1 Large cucumber**
- ◆ **1" Ginger root**

ginger root

Core
- ◆ **1 Green apple, medium size** (skin on)

Remove the strings from
- ◆ **3 stalks Celery**

Cut the above into chunks for blending.

Separate the leaves from
- ◆ **Half bunch Parsley** (to yield ¼ cup leaves)

green apple

THE JUICE

Put in a ***blender***

 ◆ The prepped cucumber, apple, celery, ginger root, and parsley leaves
 ◆ **1 cup   Baby spinach leaves** (or kale de-stemmed and torn into pieces)
 ◆ **2 cups Water**

Freshly squeeze into the blender

 ◆ **1 Tb Lemon juice (half a lemon)**

Blend until smooth, taste, and adjust. . .

Enjoy! Bottoms up!

Coconut Tea

This tea changed the life of one of my students. She was an obese attorney who had tried vainly to lose weight most of her life. She drank coconut tea as a class project, expecting yet another dismal experience. At the end of the quarter, she stood in front of the class in tears, as she reported dropping almost 20 pounds.

She had a thermos of coconut tea with her all day, sipping it whenever she got hungry. Coconut oil isn't stored in the body; it is used up as it gives energy—a shining example of eating fat to lose fat.

MAKES the number of servings you choose

When to start: 5-10 minutes before enjoying
Hands on time: 3 minutes
Stove time: Depends on how much tea water you heat up

PREP

Mise en place.

Boil or heat to the appropriate tea temperature[107] the amount of water to make the quantity of coconut tea you want.

Optional:
If you'd like hot tea to mix with coconut, **brew** your tea first.[108] Otherwise, plain hot water is fine.

In a ***serving cup, teapot or thermos***, mix as much as you plan to drink for the day in these proportions
   ♦ **1 Tb Coconut oil**
   ♦ **1 cup Hot water or brewed tea**

Taste and adjust as necessary. ***Enjoy!***

---

[107] Black, Pu-Erh, or oolong teas are best brewed at 200°F or higher; green and white teas at 170–185°F.
[108] Use tea leaves rather than tea bags, which are usually toxic. For how to brew tea, see the chapter at the end of this cookbook on kitchen tools—item 5. Tea Tools. It's just as easy as tea bags once you have the tools and know how.

Butter Tea or Coffee

Butter tea or coffee is an elixir made in heaven. It offers a gentle alertness that fuels the will to do something—be it mental or physical, analysis or exercise—and simultaneously calms down unwanted hunger signals.

This drink originated in the Tibetan Himalayas. Monks and sherpas made it with yak butter and black tea; it fueled deep meditation, unceasing chanting, and challenging treks. I'm thrilled that it found its way to the West, through Dave Asprey and his Bulletproof coffee.[109] Butter tea is my first sustenance of the day, after warm water.

If you have an immersion blender or an ordinary blender with a *glass* pitcher, you're in business. A fork doesn't create the same magic, and a blender with a plastic pitcher may leach plasticizers into the hot liquid. I most often use an immersion blender with brewed Pu-Erh or black/red tea in a metal pitcher.[110] Sometimes I shake matcha tea powder, hot water, and butter in a thermos with a matcha mixing ball.

MAKES 2 servings

When to start:	About 10 minutes before enjoying
Hands on time:	5 minutes
Stove time:	5 minutes

PREP

Mise en place.

BREW

Brew coffee or tea, as you usually make it. Use shade-grown coffee beans if possible. Or use a stronger tea, like Pu-Erh, oolong, or red/black, the highest quality you can afford, from leaves rather than tea bags. Or matcha tea powder and near-boiling water in a thermos.

---

[109] Dave adds his specific MCT oil to high quality coffee, along with the butter. More on Bulletproof coffee in the chapter on digestive resting in *Crazy Eating in the Land of Foodlike Substances*, the second Crazy Eating book.

[110] Like the pitchers baristas use to froth milk for espresso in cafés. Inexpensive "frothing pitchers" made from stainless steel are available online. A large mug works too.

BLEND
Warm the **blending pitcher or thermos** and **cup,** by pouring hot water in and out.

Add to the warmed pitcher and blend on high about a minute, or shake in a thermos
- **2 cups Brewed tea/coffee**
- **1-2 Tb Butter**

Optional:
- **1 Tb Brain Octane Oil**[111]

SERVE

Pour into a warmed cup or thermos.

Enjoy!

---

[111] Brain Octane is part of Dave Asprey's "bulletproof" formula—the C8 fraction of coconut oil that may enhance mental function.

Hot Chocolate Readymix Powder

On a cold morning or evening, or when I'm hankering for a pick-me-up, hot chocolate often appears on my radar. I can make it in just a few minutes because I always have my chocolate readymix in the pantry and cream in the fridge.

MAKES 2 cups of this magical powder—for 8 cups of liquid pleasure

When to start: 5 minutes
Hands-on time: 5 minutes
Stove time: 0 minutes

PREP

Mise en place.

In a **small bowl** mix together
- **1 cup Unsweetened cacao powder**
- **1 Tb Cinnamon powder**
- **1 Tb Turmeric powder**
- **½ tsp Salt**

Optional:
If you need added sweetness:
- **Pinch Monk fruit powder**

Put the mix in an **airtight glass or ceramic container** and store in a cool dark place.

turmeric

Enjoy whenever you want a cup of healing hot cocoa in just a few minutes!

Healing Hot Chocolate

What makes it healing? The cacao and the spices—without added sugar and milk, two risky ingredients in most every hot chocolate recipe I've seen. Watch out also for cornstarch, sometimes added to thicken the liquid. Cornstarch is a carbohydrate extracted from corn, of which 90% in the United States is grown with GMOs.

Here we use natural, raw, grass-fed cream for both thickening and flavor, optional monk fruit drops for sweetness, and a couple of spices to raise nutritive value. Enjoy this appetite-reducing healing libation without guilt!

SERVES 2

When to start:	5 minutes
Hands-on time:	5 minutes
Stove time:	0 minutes

PREP

Mise en place.

heavy cream

In a **small saucepan**, bring to a boil
- **¾ cup Water**

Mix in
- **1/3 cup Hot chocolate readymix** (see recipe)
- *Stir* in **1 cup Heavy cream**

Heat the mix, being careful not to boil it.

Optional:
For extra sweetness or fragrance, add
- **5-10 drops Monk fruit extract** for sweetness
- **1/8 tsp Vanilla extract** for fragrance

Taste and adjust.

Pour into your most beautiful cups and *enjoy!*

P.S. If you want to be extra decadent (and cool, like a barista), whip some heavy cream, swirl it on top, and dust: and/or cinnamon.

cacao powder

VARIATIONS

Mocha:
Add and mix in
- **Single or double Freshly brewed espresso shot**

Wild Mushroom Hot Chocolate:[112]
Replace 2 tablespoons of the cacao powder with
- **2 Tb Wild mushroom powder**

---

[112] Many thanks to California Bay Area nutritionist Heather Holt for the experience of this exotic libation.

Turmeric Tonic

I fell in love with turmeric tonic at a Paleo restaurant in Berkeley. It was one of their most popular beverages. When they closed down, I decided I couldn't live without it, but they had disappeared.

I searched for recipes online but they all contained some form of sugar—refined sugar, agave nectar (which is mostly unhealthy fructose), honey, or maple syrup. Some used cayenne instead of black pepper, probably not knowing that black pepper has a health function—it increases the bioavailability of turmeric. Some versions were cold, made with sparkling water, but cold food or drink uses energy to bring it up to body temperature.[113]

I did find useful info—conversion rules for spices from fresh to dried and the tip that peeling fresh turmeric or ginger is not necessary, since it will be strained …

Turmeric tonic can be stimulating, like that first morning cup of coffee or tea. Plus it's healing and out of the ordinary. You can make it really bright by using fresh roots (often available in supermarkets—if not, ask your grocer for them). Otherwise, powdered ingredients are a fallback.

TIPS

1. Wash and scrub turmeric and ginger to remove dirt. They are underground stems (rhizomes).
2. Turmeric, especially fresh, can stain. It's good to wear gloves while grating or cutting it.
3. Peeling turmeric or ginger for this recipe is not necessary because you will strain it before serving.
4. Fresh turmeric is less bitter than dried.
5. Fresh-to-dried conversion:
   - 3 tsp (1 Tb) fresh = 1 tsp dried; 2" fresh turmeric or ginger yields 1 Tb grated.

---

[113] Weight-loss plans that rely on calorie restriction recommend cold drinks because the body uses more energy to process them. But this energy is precious and needs to be used judiciously. Intelligent weight loss relies on burning body fat, not on using up energy.

MAKES 1 quart

When to start: 5-10 minutes before enjoying

Hands-on time: 3 minutes

Stove time: Depends on how much tea water you heat up.

PREP

Mise en place.

Juice into a ***small saucepan***
- ◆ **1 Lemon**, yielding 1–2 Tb juice
- ◆ Cut leftover lemon shell into 8 pieces and add to the saucepan.

Grate[114] (skip if using powders)
- ◆ **4" piece Turmeric root**[115]
- ◆ **3" piece Ginger root**[116]

lemon

COOK

Add to the saucepan with the lemon
- ◆ **1 quart Water**
- ◆ **10-30 drops Monk fruit extract**
- ◆ **¼ - 1 tsp Black pepper, freshly ground**[117]

The grated
- ◆ **Turmeric and ginger**
- ◆ (OR 2 Tb turmeric powder + 1 Tb ginger powder)

Bring it to a simmer over medium-to-medium high.

Simmer 3 minutes while stirring gently.

---

[114] There are several tools for grating, all of which are at the ready—a food processor with grating attachment, a microplane, a round "box grater" with a solid bottom to catch the grated food, a garlic press, and a mortar and pestle. Each has its unique advantage depending on the task at hand. You will soon discover which to use for what … For this recipe I used my food processor, because both roots are relatively hard and I was doing a substantial quantity.

[115] Technically "rhizome" but commonly called a root.

[116] Technically "rhizome" but commonly called a root. Ok to skip the ginger, just add equivalent quantity of fresh turmeric.

[117] Black pepper greatly enhances the bioavailability of turmeric.

Taste and adjust. If too strong, add hot water. If too weak, simmer longer. If too sweet, add turmeric. If not sweet enough, add monk fruit extract a couple of drops at a time.

SERVE

Strain into serving mugs, glasses, or pitcher.

Optional:
Mix in heavy cream or homemade kefir to taste.

Enjoy!

STORE

Leftover tonic keeps in the fridge indefinitely. Warm it up to drink.

Store unused rhizomes either in a glass jar in the fridge (several days) or in the freezer. OR to last a year or more, pack them in a glass jar, cover with vodka and refrigerate.

Power Smoothie

I've been drinking power smoothies for over 30 years now—either for my first or last meal of the day. They've gone through many iterations … these are the three versions I use now.

My power smoothies are my health insurance policy. Every ingredient in them is a nutrient powerhouse:

- kefir[118] (probiotics, protein, CLA and minerals);
- cod liver oil (omega 3s and vitamin A);
- brain-enhancing medium chain triglyceride (MCT) oil, a component of coconut oil;
- black seed oil brimming with antioxidants;
- mint and basil, promoting digestion and immune health; etc.

mint *basil*

Following are three variations on the smoothie formula, each made in under five minutes from start to drinking—assuming you have your very own kefir in your fridge.

---

[118] Kefir is a fermented milk drink made by immersing kefir bacteria in milk. Kefir originated in the Caucasus mountains of Eastern Europe and Russia. Marilyn the Kefir Lady (kefirlady.com) sells the bacteria by mail within the United States. She sells the real McCoy—descendants of Caucasus kefir bacteria. If you keep them fed, they will multiply and keep you well supplied with kefir. Some of mine are now 11 years old!

VARIATION 1: HERBY SMOOTHIE, WITH FRESH MINT AND BASIL

PREP

Mise en place.

Heat water to just under boiling (200˚ F in my Cuisinart *water kettle*).
To a *blender*, add

- ¾ cup Mineral water[119] or kombucha[120]
- ½ cup Long-fermented kefir from raw milk[121]
- ¼ cup Oil mix (2-4 cups mix made in advance): 2 Tb cod liver oil[122] + 1 Tb Brain Octane oil[123] + 1 Tb black seed oil
- Handful Mint leaves
- Handful Basil leaves
- ½ cup Hot water

Optional—if *not* trying to burn fat/lose weight:

- ½ Banana, medium size
- ¼ cup Strawberries (least carby), blueberries, peach, or other

Blend about a minute, until all ingredients disintegrate into the smoothie.
Taste and adjust if necessary:

- If too cold, add hot water; If too hot, add ice cube.
- If too thick, add mineral water or kombucha.
- If too sour, add a few drops of **monk fruit extract**.

---

[119] The Mountain Valley is the only sparkling water I have found that is naturally sourced and has more magnesium than calcium. Gerolsteiner has equal percentages of the two minerals; others have more calcium which we don't need as much because we typically consume more of it than magnesium.

[120] If you want to lose weight, do not use most commercial kombuchas, which are flavored with fruit juice.

[121] See recipe below "Your Very Own Kefir" on how to make long fermented kefir. It's worth it!

[122] I use Carlson lemon cod liver oil. I could not get used to the taste of fermented cod liver oil, which has even more nutrition.

[123] Dave Asprey's Bulletproof MCT oil

VARIATION 2: SPICY SMOOTHIE, WITH OR WITHOUT ADDED PROTEIN

Follow the recipe above, except, instead of fresh mint and basil, add
- **1 Tb CMT smoothie readymix:**[124] 2 parts cinnamon + 1 part moringa + 1 part turmeric

Optional: For people who don't eat much meat, add
- **1 Tb Protein powder**[125]

VARIATION 3: CHOCOLATE SMOOTHIE

Follow the recipe above, except, instead of fresh mint and basil or the CMT readymix, add
- **1 Tb Cacao powder**

Optional: For people who don't eat much meat, add
- **1 Tb Protein powder**[126]

SERVE

Pour into a **big glass or mug.**
Enjoy the smoothie you chose today!

Note: Once you know what you like, make your own smoothie readymixes and you'll have your favorite smoothies in minutes any time you want.

---

[124] It's important to buy herbs from a trusted herb store, like Lhasa Karnak in Berkeley and American Botanical Pharmacy in Los Angeles, California.
[125] Dr. Axe's Collagen Protein Powder is a good brand.
[126] Dr. Axe's Collagen Protein Powder is a good brand.

Your Very Own Kefir [127]

Why make your own kefir when it's sold in grocery stores at very reasonable prices?

Because, first, commercial kefir has too much sugar. Even the highest-quality plain kefir[128] is not fermented enough—the kefir bacteria are taken off their job of eating lactose before they've consumed it all. After all, the more lactose left in the kefir, the sweeter (less sour) it tastes. At home, you can let your micro-pets eat to their heart's content. You can always taste each day or adjust an overly sour taste with a healthy non-sugar sweetener.

The second reason to make kefir at home is to avoid inadvertently buying kefir with disagreeable ingredients—thickeners, preservatives, sugar, flavors or fruit. An organic kefir I saw on Amazon.com listed these ingredients: "organic strawberries, organic cane sugar, natural flavors, organic locust bean gum, pectin, fruit and vegetable juice for color." No matter how organic sugar or fruits are, sugar is sugar. "Natural flavors" are anything but natural after they emerge from the lab, and fruit juice is liquid fructose, the most damaging sugar.

A third reason to make your own: You can choose what kind of milk to ferment—raw, not pasteurized; goat's, sheep's or camel's milk;[129] whole, not low-fat.

Homemade kefir provides protein and excellent fats that support fat burning while building lean muscle. In contrast, protein smoothies usually use protein powder instead —a highly processed extract of milk, eggs or certain plants[130]—considered (erroneously) a health boost and muscle builder. Many such powders contain heavy metals (e.g. lead, arsenic, mercury), BPA and other known toxicants, reports the Harvard Medical School.[131]

This recipe gives you recommended proportions of milk to kefir grains. You choose how much to actually make.

When to start: Several days before enjoying
Hands-on time: 3 minutes
Stove time: 0 minutes

---

[127] Based on directions by Marilyn the Kefirlady—kefirlady.com—and my own experience making kefir nonstop since October 2008.

[128] For example, the Organic Pastures brand

[129] Cow's milk molecules are five times larger than goat's, and consequently not as easy to digest. Goat's milk is a boon to those with fragile digestion.

[130] Soybeans, peas, rice, potatoes or hemp.

[131] https://www.health.harvard.edu/staying-healthy/the-hidden-dangers-of-protein-powders

PREP

Mise en place.

Put kefir grains in a **clean glass jar large enough** to hold 5 to 10 times as much milk as grains. For example,

- ¼ cup (4 Tb) Kefir grains[132]
- 1¼-2½ cups Milk[133]

Cover jar with **paper towel, cheesecloth or napkin,** so that the grains can breathe. Hold the cover in place with a **rubber band or the ring of a mason jar cover.**

Leave at room temperature for 24 hours or longer. The longer the fermentation, the less lactose (milk sugar) and the more sour the kefir. Fermentation time varies with season, sunlight, and ambient temperature. Several days is not unusual.

During fermentation, the grains tend to gather at the top. Swirl the jar or stir the contents gently with a **non-metal[134] utensil** several times during the fermentation period, to distribute them more evenly.

The kefir is ready when you see a translucent band or patches of liquid across the jar, anywhere in the jar. Stir it and let it sit longer to ensure maximum elimination of sugar. You'll see the clear whey form again. If the amount of clear whey doesn't increase, your kefir pets have done their job. It can take a day or several days, depending on your ambient temperature. If you want to slow fermentation down to a crawl, put the jar in the fridge and the little guys will go to sleep.

When the fermentation is done, stir gently and strain the kefir through a **non-metal colander** into a **bowl.** Transfer the kefir to a **glass bottle.**[135]

Welcome to real kefir! Enjoy by itself or in a smoothie!

STORAGE

You don't need to use a clean jar each time; the jar you fermented the kefir in does not get dirty, just kefir-y—clumps of kefir start collecting in the neck and bottom of the jar.

---

[132] Real kefir grains are available from Marilyn the Kefir Lady at http://kefirlady.com.

[133] Ideally, use RAW (unpasteurized) milk. Do NOT use ultrapasteurized milk. Vat-pasteurized milk is the best of the pasteurized. Goat's or sheep's milk is easier to digest than cow's milk, as is camel's milk, but camel's milk is not commonly available and is relatively expensive. Next best is milk from Jersey, Guernsey or Asian cows; yaks; or donkeys. Find a source of the best milk in your area at http://www.realmilk.com.

[134] Kefir bacteria do not like metal.

[135] You can also scoop out the grains and transfer the grains to a new jar, keeping the kefir in the original soaking jar.

I have stored kefir grains in the fridge or freezer for several weeks … The grains multiply over time. When you have excess, give them away or sell them, or, if you don't mind eating your pets, put them in your smoothies!

kefir grains

P.S. I have been tending my kefir pets since October 2008. I got them from the Kefir Lady, who has a goat farm in Michigan USA. She affirms the grains have descended from real Caucasus Mountains bacteria and, with proper care, they should "last forever."

Since the beginning, I have fed my kefir pets fresh, unpasteurized goat's milk from Evergreen Acres Dairy, Tres Pinos, CA, with whom I had a goat herd-sharing agreement. Then in 2015 Evergreen was certified in California as a raw milk dairy and its milk now appears in retail stores. I also use Organic Pastures raw cow's milk.

Basic Bone Broth

For years, every two weeks, I made bone broth. I don't anymore because I have finally found a local supplier of real, 100% grass fed/pastured broth.[136] I store the broth in the coldest part of my fridge—the back section of the lowest shelf—where it stays good for at least a month.

"Broth" and "stock" are used here interchangeably to mean the liquid made from cooking bones, meat, and/or vegetables. It can be used as a warm drink first thing in the morning (or any time), or as the base of a soup, braise, gravy, or sauce. Grains—if you still eat them—are more flavorful and nutritious when cooked in bone broth, or half broth half water, instead of just water.

Don't be tempted to use bouillon cubes—they are filled with unhealthy additives, and very little, if any, bone stock.[137]

This recipe was inspired by Sally Fallon Morell's account of how to make beef broth, in her now classic book *Nourishing Traditions*.[138] She recommends using three kinds of bones: knuckle bones and feet, marrow bones, and rib and neck bones for their different benefits.[139] I use whatever bones are available, including chicken bones and carcasses, and any beef or pork bones I've saved in my freezer from bone-y meals.

MAKES about 4 quarts

When to start:	A couple of days before enjoying
Hands-on time:	3 minutes
Stove time:	0 minutes

---

[136] Scott Brennan, owner of and chief chef at Fifth Quarter Charcuterie in Oakland, California.

[137] Ingredients listed in British "Oxo cubes" are: "wheat flour, salt, yeast extract, cornflour, colouring, flavor enhancers (monosodium glutamate), beef fat, flavouring, dried beef bonestock, sugar, onion, pepper extract."
Ingredients listed in Wylie's chicken flavored bouillon cubes:
No bone stock at all. Instead, a nightmarish collection of additives: salt, sugar, mechanically separated cooked ground chicken meat, sodium bicarbonate, monosodium glutamate, hydrolyzed corn gluten, corn maltodextrin, onion powder, chicken fat, hydrolyzed corn gluten protein, partially hydrogenated soybean oil and partially hydrogenated cottonseed oil, autolyzed yeast extract, water, garlic powder, disodium inosinate and disodium guanylate, dextrose, cooked chicken powder, natural chicken flavor, hydrolyzed soy protein, calcium silicate, gelatin, soy lecithin, natural flavor, turmeric, corn syrup solids, spice, modified cornstarch, silicon dioxide, diacetyl (flavor), artificial flavor, tricalcium phosphate, alpha tocopherols (antioxidant), corn oil, BHA (preservative) propyl gallate, citric acid BHT (preservative).

[138] Fifteen years later, in 2014, Sally wrote a broth sequel, *Nourishing Broth,* on the astounding and numerous benefits of bone broth.

[139] Knuckle bones and feet for gelatin; marrow bones for flavor and certain nutrients, including CLA for fat burn, muscle and blood building, and cancer prevention; rib and neck bones for added color and flavor.

PREP

Mise en place.

Cut each head in half to expose the flesh of
- ◆ **1-2 heads Garlic**

Cut into 4 pieces
- ◆ **1 large Onion, yellow or red, or leek/scallion**

Let the garlic and onion sit for 10 minutes or more.

beef marrow

Cut into 1-inch pieces
- ◆ **3-4 Carrots**

In a *large stock pot or crockpot*, put:
- ◆ **6 lbs. Bones**[140]
- ◆ **1/4 cup Vinegar or lemon juice**[141]
- ◆ **2 Handfuls Fresh herbs: Bay leaves, thyme, rosemary, basil,** etc.[142]
- ◆ **1 tsp Salt**[143]
- ◆ **4+ quarts Water**—to cover the bones and herbs

Let the pot sit for an hour off heat, or bring to a simmer on medium low (takes about an hour). This allows the vinegar or lemon juice to start drawing out minerals from the bones.

As the liquid begins to simmer, scum will rise to the top. Skim it. [144]

Keep stock on a bare simmer 8-12 hours. Turn it off overnight and simmer another 8-12 hours the next day. And so on, for a total simmering time of 16-72 hours. The lower range is for chicken, the higher for beef, the middle for pork and lamb. Add water as needed to keep the bones covered.

---

[140] Bones are available at farmers markets or online at U.S. Wellness Meats and Tropical Traditions. You can also use bones left from meat you have cooked and eaten—beef, pork, lamb, chicken, etc.
[141] To enhance the extraction of minerals from the bones.
[142] Can use dried herbs: 3 bay leaves, total of 2 Tb other herbs.
[143] This is a relatively small amount to allow for customized salting in making sauces and gravies. To use stock as a beverage, I just grind some salt into the stock when I heat it.
[144] Scum produced by simmering stock is protein denatured by heat. It is not harmful and has no flavor, but neither is it beneficial. If left in, it turns the stock gray and cloudy.

Optional: About 10 minutes before finish, add
 ◆ **1 bunch Parsley**

Cool the stock enough to handle.

Strain the stock through a **china cap or other big strainer** into a **large bowl** ideally with a lip to make pouring easier.

Pour into **quart mason jars**, cool down to room temp and store in fridge. Quart-size wide-mouth jars are the most versatile. The stock gels and the fat rises and forms a "fat cap," which protects the broth and allows storage in the fridge for several weeks.

If you are drinking the stock straight or using it to make soup, just heat and add salt to taste. If you are using it to make sauce, remove the fat cap (which lessens the broth flavor). Save the fat in a glass jar or **stainless steel container** labeled with date and type of fat, e.g., "Chicken 9/15/10."

Refrigerate or freeze depending on how fast you will use it.

Enjoy!

My Favorite Kitchen Tools [145]

There are implements, gadgets and small appliances that save immense time and effort in the kitchen—and help us make healthy, budget-friendly, delicious food. I use the ones on this list almost every day. They're simpler than electronic gadgets, just as indispensable, and have no negative side effects.

1. Food Scoop

My long-time kitchen friend is almost 30 years old. Its wooden handle is smooth, like a worn piano bench.

I bought it at a small kitchenware store in San Francisco. I was browsing, looking longingly at merchandise I couldn't afford. I was the only one in the store and the kindly saleswoman came over to me from behind the counter. Before I could blurt out that I was only window shopping, she beamed at me and said, "I have something for you that you will use more than anything else in your kitchen." She stretched her arm out, with this unassuming thing on the palm of her hand.

I stared. "What is it?" I asked at last.

---

[145] This chapter is reprinted here—with the addition of the "spider" tool— from the second Crazy Eating book: *Crazy Eating in the Land of Foodlike Substances*—for readers who don't yet have that book.

"It's a food scoop," she said. "You use it to pick up anything you've chopped, so you can plop it all in your pot, including the little bits, in just one or two moves ... Like this ..." And she took me to the counter, where she deftly wielded the scoop.

It was quite different from what I had been doing—bringing the cutting board to the pot on the stove and carefully sliding, say, chopped veggies into the pot, hoping they'd all make it in. Or scooping them with my hands into the pot, then having to wipe my hands off before grabbing a cooking spoon to stir.

The scoop cost less than the ten-dollar bill I had in my purse that day, and now it has its own reserved place on my drain board, always ready for action, a friend for life. It has helped make food prep the breeze I need it to be, to stick to my health and budget-friendly eating day in and day out. There are several online to choose from.

2. Sharpening Rods[146]

These make me feel like a real chef. I use them to keep my knives sharp, which makes cutting food a delight. Swipe, swipe, swipe, swipe, swipe, swipe. That's it!

The tool mimics what a chef does each time he or she starts using a knife. Chefs use a "steel"—a honing steel rod against which they swipe the knife blade. Why? Because the stainless steel at the cutting edge of a knife dulls with each use—it spreads microscopically, especially when hitting a cutting board again and again and again. Swiping the edge of the blade against the steel rod realigns the edge, tamping back any spreading that may have occurred and keeping the knives razor sharp for a very long time.

The white rods are for ordinary people who don't have the practiced hand of a chef. We don't need to learn how to hold a honing steel so we don't cut off a finger, or how to angle the knife just so. The rods are made of smooth white ceramic, each about 9 inches long and a little less than ¼ inch in diameter. They're loosely inserted in two small holes, about ¼ inch deep, at one end of a polished wooden slab 2 inches wide x 9 inches long. The holes are located so that when the rods are inserted, they slide into the correct angle.

---

[146] https://agrussell.com/knife/A-G-Russell-Ceramic-Sharpener--CS94

Then all I have to do is grab the knife, blade down, and—starting close to the handle—swipe down one rod, then swipe down the other. Three pairs of swipes, six seconds; that's it. Chopping onions, garlic and carrots, slicing meat, cutting really anything becomes a breeze ...

I found my ceramic rods through Eric Weiss, a knife-sharpening craftsman at the Berkeley Farmers Market who sharpens knives for market customers. I had brought all my knives to him—paying about $100 for 10 knives. When I asked him for tips on how to maintain my knives, he gave me the name of A.G. Russell, a passionate maker of knives in the U.S. Deep South[147] for over 50 years.

I watched the guru's videos and knew he was a master. I happily bought the knife sharpener you see in the image—the "white rods," one of A.G. Russell's most popular tools.

3. Two Cutting Boards

Wielding knives requires a good cutting board. Like almost everything these days, there's an array of different kinds, from traditional maple hardwood to foldable plastic.
If you enjoy browsing, go to *The Spruce* website[148] and check out the whole array.
Otherwise, here's what I recommend: Two cutting boards, one for meat, poultry and fish; the other for everything else. The big distinction is the greater need for prompt cleaning of the board for meat, poultry and fish. I do it immediately after use, whereas I leave the general board for my final cleanup at the end of the day. I clean both boards with dishwashing soap and hot water.

---

[147] Rogers, Arkansas, the location of the first Walmart and ranked by CNN No. 10 of the 100 fastest-growing cities in the U.S.
[148] Anthony Irizarry, "The 7 Best Cutting Boards to Buy in 2019," December 12, 2018, https://www.thespruce.com/best-cutting-boards-4067664

My "everything else" cutting board is made of bamboo. It's the most durable material, even more durable than oak or other hardwood, and there's no chance of plastic contamination.[149] It's 14" x 11 ¼" and ¾" thick—light enough for me to handle easily, yet sturdy enough to withstand chopping anything. I have two other bamboo boards made of the same material, but half the width, that I use to cut and serve cheese and other hors d'oeuvres.

The meat board should look different—easily distinguishable from your everything-else board. It can be smaller or bigger or have a different grain or wood color. Mine is smaller (12 ¼" x 9 ¼" and ¾" thick) AND made of maple hardwood with reddish brown strips alternating with blond. It's the first chopping board I ever bought; I've had it for decades, yet it looks almost new.

When plastic cutting boards first came out, I got a few. But they started looking pretty awful very quickly. I wondered about plastic bits going into the food ... I discarded them and went back to my trusty, beautiful wooden boards.

You might wonder which is easier to clean and keep free of bacteria from food. Some thought plastic, but studies in the late 1980s by Dean Cliver, a researcher at the University of California, Davis, and top expert on cutting board food safety, found no difference between wood and plastic in terms of cleanliness. Just go for bamboo or maple, which are fine grained—not cypress, which has wider grooves in which bacteria could thrive.

Make a specific space to store your cutting boards and they will easily become a part of your daily kitchen rituals. There's a special place *inside* my drain board (aka dish drying rack) for my cutting boards to dry after washing. If placed outside, directly on the drain mat, water collects at the point of contact with the mat and that part of the board becomes slimy and dark, a sign of beginning mold.

To store my cutting boards, I use a bookend at one end of a large lazy Susan in a cabinet under a kitchen counter. The bookend slips easily left or right, closing or opening up space as I take out or insert a board.

Don't get seduced by the lively colors of plastic cutting boards. Plastic leaching into the food is a big risk. Besides, a traditional wooden cutting board makes you feel solid in the kitchen, even when you're fumbling around with a new recipe.

I've had my wooden cutting boards for decades; they are true workhorses.

---

[149] Plastic may be lighter and more easily stored, but it introduces the risk of plastic contamination. It's actually easy to store wooden cutting boards—once you have a place for them.

4. Electric Water Kettle

What's the first thing that crosses your lips in the morning? For me, it's a big glass of warm (almost hot) water, often with a squirt of lemon or lime. I feel like it washes away the debris of the night, leaving my insides clear and ready for new food.

My partner wakes up before I do and fills our stainless steel hot water kettle. All I have to do is push the "start" button and I have hot water in a few minutes.

My kettle[150] is indispensable throughout the day. I use it to warm every glass of water I drink[151] and to brew loose-leaf tea. The Cuisinart kettle has six different water temperatures, allowing me to use precise temps for each of the teas I drink: 175° F for green, 185° for white, 200° for oolong, and "boil" for black, red or Pu-erh. And it keeps the water at the target temp for 30 minutes.

Warm water and hot tea are my hot buttons, and my water kettle makes them quick, easy and satisfying.

5. Tea Tools

- **Tea Master.**

My tea master is a glass teapot with a strainer top that makes about a cup and a half (12 ounces/400 grams) of tea. I learned about tea masters from Winnie Yu, an accomplished tea connoisseur whose tea was voted among the world's top ten by National Geographic.[152]

---

[150] Cuisinart brand
[151] According to Ayurveda, traditional medicine from India, warm water requires the least energy for the body to process. It's closest to body temperature.
[152] The tea is sold at Teance, a beautiful Berkeley tea shop Winnie created in 2006.

I make green and white teas in my tea master with the following method: Warm the vessel by pouring hot water in and out (back into the kettle) . Fill the tea master with 175° F water for green or 185° F for white, sprinkle a heaping tablespoon and a half of loose tea leaves into the water, wait 45 seconds in stillness, and it's done.

- **Tea Tray**

It's the shallow rectangular wooden box with a slatted removable top, under the cup and teapots in the photos. A tea tray catches inevitable water spills or the rinsing water poured over a Yixing teapot to develop its radiance. (See below.)

- **Yixing Teapots**

I have three, each devoted to just one type of tea. Yixing clay, from eastern China, where it's been used to make teapots since the 10th century, retains the flavor of the tea brewed in it. That's why I dedicate each pot to one tea type: one for oolong, one for black or red tea, and one for Pu-erh. These teas have more complex and robust flavors, which a Yixing clay pot preserves and deepens with use.

Tip: How to give your Yixing teapot a special shine: This may seem weird, but here's how you do it: Put tea leaves in the pot. Pour hot water (about 200° F) to just cover the leaves. Cover the pot and immediately pour out the water through a strainer into another cup. Pour more hot water to fill the teapot. Cover the pot and pour the rinsing water over the pot, which is sitting on a bamboo tea tray that catches the water. Over time, regular rinsing will give your Yixing teapot a special shine, like an inner radiance.

• **Tea Spoon**

This is a lovely wooden spoon tea aficionados use to scoop tea out of a bag or canister into a pot. The "bowl" of this spoon is wider and longer than a regular teaspoon, shaped more like a mini shovel than a spoon. It is ideal for scooping dried tea leaves into a teapot, its only function.

• **Ceramic Tea Strainer**

I suppose any small strainer could do, but I got this one because I love my morning tea ritual and this strainer is part of the ritual. It's handmade with extra-fine mesh, by a local artisan. It fits nicely over my little teacup and over all my thermoses. I use it first to strain out bits of tea dust from the tea-rinsing water, then to catch fine bits in steeped tea as I pour it into a cup or thermos.

• **Stanley Thermos.**

It keeps liquids hot for longer than most thermoses. And it's great for "thermos tea," a time-saver for people who like to bring delicious hot tea on the go with them, like me. I learned it from an extreme tea aficionado,[153] who learned it from a Chinese tea master.

First you get a Stanley Master Series thermos (mine is 20 ounces). Warm it by filling a third of it with very hot water and letting it sit, closed, for about three minutes. Pour the water out and repeat the warming process twice more. Scoop a tablespoon of a robust type of tea—oolong, Pu-erh, red, or black—into the thermos, rinse the tea leaves, and then let the wet leaves sit in the closed thermos about five minutes. Fill the thermos with water at the right temperature—190° F for oolong, 205° F for Pu-erh, boiling for red/black.[154] Let it steep a minute, then start sipping and enjoy it hot all day.

---

[153] Jim Conwell, Berkeley psychotherapist. Jim is aging a big stash of Pu-erh tea in Hong Kong, because the climate is ideal there for the optimal aging of tea.
[154] Tea called "black" in the West is called "red" in China.

The Stanley thermos, warmed in this way, holds the heat for about 12 hours—as I experienced firsthand when my "monkey picked tieguanyin" tea in my Stanley thermos remained hot and delicious all day.

6. Espresso Machine[155] and Grinder[156]

They were a birthday gift to my partner and have contributed much to the kitchen ambience. Even the messiness of the coffee grounds on the counter feels cozy. The grinder puts out grounds to exact specs and the espresso machine froths cream and makes espresso just as fast as they do in cafés. It's fun to have excellent coffee and tea at home and feel like you're in a café

---

[155] Breville brand
[156] Encore brand

7. Steamer

If you eat veggies every day or need to warm up leftovers quickly, a steamer pot (or Instant Pot; it steams too) becomes important.

Steaming veggies is almost always my first step in cooking them, from chard to carrots. After washing and prepping, I steam them for 5-10 minutes; season them with salt and one of my savory spice mixes, and toss them with butter, olive oil or walnut oil.

I also use my steamer to warm up food. In just a few minutes, the food is hot and still moist, as it was when first cooked. I don't use a microwave,[157] and I've discovered that heating up leftovers in the oven dries them out. They'd have to be wrapped in parchment with some liquid to prevent drying. So I just throw them in the steamer; they never get dry and always taste fresh. It sometimes makes baked foods even juicier than when they were first cooked.

I used to use a steamer basket in a regular pot, but the metal rod that sticks out from the center of the basket[158] was a pain. A pot designed for steaming is much easier to use. It has an unobstructed basket that you can remove easily.

A steamer pot can double up as a regular pot for general use—but in my kitchen it's rarely available for anything else.

8. Instant Pot

I'm falling in love ... The Pot does my three favorite methods well: slow cooking, sautéing, and steaming, and it has introduced me to pressure cooking. I've never owned a pressure cooker, always having been wary of their intense force.

---

[157] I don't use a microwave, even just to heat food, because a review of relevant research indicates that microwave radiation distorts food molecules, which may become carcinogenic. At the very least, the continuous bombardment of the food by subatomic particles could lessen, if not obliterate, its nutrition. See Dr. Mercola, "How Your Microwave Oven Damages Your Health In Multiple Ways,"
https://articles.mercola.com/sites/articles/archive/2010/05/18/microwave-hazards.aspx
[158] which is used for removing the basket when the steaming is done

But one day I was in a huge hurry, and all I had to make for dinner was a raw pastured chicken that had been sitting in my fridge several days. Into the Pot it went with Himalayan salt[159] and a couple of quarts of farmer-made pastured poultry broth. Half an hour later, there it was—the most succulent chicken falling off the bone I had ever had. We named it Exploder Chicken—but not because it actually exploded, thank goodness; I had followed the Pot directions ever so carefully, afraid it would explode any minute with the pressure.

I haven't yet tried to boil eggs (I have a simple, fail-safe egg cooker) in the Pot, make yogurt (too much natural sugar), or bake a cake (yikes!); and I don't eat grains and beans. But if all I do is slow cook, pressure cook and sauté (I like my old fashioned steamer), the Pot is worth every dollar I paid for it!

9. Slow Cooker/Crockpot and Wonderbag

If you don't have an Instant Pot, a slow cooker/crockpot or Wonderbag work beautifully. They cook food ever so gently over many hours and produce succulent, falling-off-the-bone meat and poultry. A crockpot uses electricity and allows more adjustments during cooking than an Instant Pot. A Wonderbag, made with beautiful rural African fabric, uses electricity only the first fifteen minutes, after which the food continues cooking for eight or more hours from the heat kept in by the bag's amazing insulation. I used them both for years.

---

[159] I did not add the usual herbs and spices because I had just started my Carnivore Diet experiment and was off all plant foods.

10. Air Fryer OR Countertop Convection Oven OR Toaster Oven

I didn't buy my air fryer to "crisp and flavor food like a deep fryer but without the fat" as promised in ads. (I'm a firm believer in fat, as you know.) I use my air fryer to do everything I did with my countertop convection oven, which was falling apart after some 25 years of constant cooking. I've never used my regular oven, as it's unnecessarily big; it just provides convenient storage for pot lids. My much smaller air fryer, which has a similar footprint on the counter as its predecessor toaster oven,[160] does the cooking. Everything I'd cook in an oven fits in the countertop (now air fryer), so why waste the electrical energy on heating a larger oven?

I've roasted a pork belly and a whole chicken, and baked fish in it. I crisp Cult crackers and use it as a warming oven for plates and prepared food. In just a few minutes, an almond croissant (which I indulge in only on Anything Goes Day) smells and tastes like it just came out of a baker's oven, even if it's been sitting in the freezer for a month. Soon, I'll do coriander-crusted roast beef in my air fryer, per Ben Mims, contributor to the *Wall Street Journal*'s "Off Duty" section and air fryer cookbook author.[161]

Delicious cooking aside, if you've been eating food deep fried in vegetable oil, like French fries or chicken, an air fryer might be just the medicine you need for pesky ailments …

11. Tongs

I have five pairs of tongs, all stainless steel, three long and two short. One of the long ones has rubber hands and is great for tossing salad. I use tongs, especially the short ones, almost every time I cook—to pick up, turn over and toss food—chops, steaks, veggies, pancakes, *tostones*, etc.

---

[160] It's just a bit deeper and taller
[161] Ben Mims, *Air Fry Every Day: 75 Recipes to Fry, Roast and Bake Using Your Air Fryer.*

12. Two Graters

One has a single coarse grating surface and hangs by its rubber handle on a hook on the side of a butcher block island. Long ago, it replaced a bulky unsightly box grater, saving precious storage space. I usually use it to grate cheese for an omelet or a salad, sometimes to grate the zest of limes or lemons to spike up veggies or smoothies. Cleaning this grater is effortless—just tap it sharply on a cutting board to shake off crumbs, or pass it under hot running water and return it to its hook to dry.

The second is a grating bucket from the MoMA[162] design store catalog. It's no art piece—it looks just like a box grater except it's round, without a handle, and, most importantly, has a bottom that holds the grated food. Think that helpful bottom makes it worth four times as much as a regular box grater?

13. Mandoline

My mandoline is a simple one-blade, one-width tool. There are others with several blades and several widths, but I found them too bulky and complicated.

I use it to slice vegetables thinly—cucumbers, zucchini, carrots, radishes. The super-thin slices elevate the experience of eating the vegetables. I dress the cucumbers with rice vinegar, a bit of dill, and a sprinkling of salt. I sauté-toss the zucchini with salt and minced garlic for just a few minutes. I dip the carrots in *gomasio* and coat radish slices in tempered butter and flaky salt, as I learned to do in France with whole breakfast radishes. Mmm.

---

[162] Museum of Modern Art

14. Blender with Glass Pitcher

After using a Vitamix for many years, I decided to buy an Oster. Why? Its pitcher is made of glass, while the Vitamix's is plastic. I still make room-temperature smoothies in the Vitamix, but I make hot Bulletproof tea and purée hot soup in the Oster—heat greatly increases the risk of plastic leaching into the food. (See the first Crazy Eating book, *Crazy Eating: What Should I Eat?* for more on this topic.)

15. Spatter Screen

It's a light, round, stainless steel screen that fits perfectly over my skillets (get one that fits your biggest skillet). It protects you from getting hit with hot oil leaping out of the pan and keeps counters free of grease and mess whenever you brown or sauté anything. Saves a ton of cleanup time!

16. Stock Strainer, Restaurant Quality

It's a sturdy, stainless steel cone 9 inches in diameter and a foot high, with lots of small holes all over. It has a curved piece attached to the outside of the wide edge that holds it in place in a 6-quart stock pot. It came from a bistro-deli in Aspen, Colorado that I co-owned for a few months many years ago. When we sold it (after learning that restaurant work was not for us), I kept this strainer and several soup ladles. Some 30 years later, they continue to grace the mesh board over my stove where I hang spatulas, ladles, and other utensils.

I make stock from veggie and herb scraps and bones I save and freeze. When the stock is done and has cooled, I put the strainer in another 6-quart pot and pour in the stock—veggies, herbs, bones and all. I press what's in the strainer with a sturdy ladle to get every last drop of precious stock, then dump the whole mess into my compost bin. Phew! My editor Laila feeds it to her dog—after crushing up the bones to make sure they were cooked long enough to be completely soft.

If you make stock regularly, it might be worth checking out a restaurant supplier for a restaurant-quality strainer.

17. Kitchen Scissors

I love using my kitchen scissors. The two blades come apart, so I can clean them easily. But the best part is their precision. In open position, one blade fits perfectly on top of the other, via an ingenious nut-and-bolt thingie in the center. When you close them, they click shut with a firm, clean sound. And the rubber handles are comfortable.

The scissors help me do a number of things:

- Snip herbs instead of mincing them.
- Cut through the membranes holding the lobes of chicken livers together.
- Cut through chicken skin or joints when cutting up whole chicken.
- Cut through fish skin when cutting fish fillets into smaller slices.
- Cut up bacon.
- Dice cooked chicken for tacos.[163]

18. Mason Jars

About 30 glass. are in circulation in my kitchen—mostly quart sized, some pint and cup sized, and a couple half-gallon ones. I store prepped veggies, leftovers, strawberries, and fresh spearmint leaves in them, instead of using plastic wrap. I ferment sour cream and kefir in them. And my stock supplier fills 12 up every three or four weeks. A few more contain stock that I make when enough vegetable trimmings and bones have accumulated in my freezer.

I buy plastic lids to replace the jars' metal ones that, unfortunately, rust after a while. The food in the jars rarely touches the lid, so I don't worry about plastic leaching. (In the rare case it does, I shield the food with waxed paper.) These lids are among the few plastic things I use.

---

[163] The last two items are from my editor, Laila, who is also a cooking aficionado and foodie.

19. Kitchen Scale

I use it to weigh food and tea. I weigh food when recipes use grams or ounces instead of cups and spoons. And I weigh loose-leaf tea that I don't use regularly or that I've just begun using—the others I can measure by feel. The right amount is usually 4 or 5 grams per eight-ounce cup of tea, but the volume of tea differs, depending on whether they're big or little leaves; rolled "pearls," like oolong; or chunks broken off a brick or wheel, like Pu-erh.

I've had my kitchen scale for decades, and it looks like new despite constant use. It has its own special place, on a shelf below my butcher block on wheels.

20. Spider

No, it's not my kitchen mascot. It's a cool tool, great for skimming the foam off stock generated while cooking, and for removing food from its cooking liquid, especially large pieces like chicken legs or prawns. It's a shallow *wide*-mesh wire strainer with a long wooden handle—in contrast to a sieve (this page), a deeper, bowl-shaped, *fine*-mesh wire strainer with a shorter metal handle (Spider photo following page).

Colander

A colander, also a strainer, is more like a plastic bowl with holes in it to remove liquid from solid pieces of food, as when you strain stock through a colander and discard the bones or carcass.

Spider

The spider got its name from its wire mesh pattern that looks like a spider's web. I used it more often when I made my own stock, to skim it.[164] Now I buy stock from a charcutier[165] who makes it from pastured poultry and sells it for less than I'd spend to make it myself!

These days I use my spider when I make Exploder Chicken (see recipe) or a big pot of bollito misto.[166]

---

[164] I still make vegetable stock when I've accumulated enough scraps to make a big pot. I strain the stock with a restaurant-grade strainer   description and photo in Item 16 of this section.

[165] A charcutier is someone who makes ground meat products like sausage, pâtés., galantines, terrines, rilletes— French creations collectively called "charcuterie" and traditionally sold in a shop dedicated to it.

[166] Bollito misto is slow-cooked boiled beef that comes to us from Italy. It is made with the tougher parts of the animal, such as shanks, tail, tongue, short ribs, and chuck, the shoulder area.

21. Chinese Soup Spoons

These porcelain spoons are last but not least. We have many. I use one virtually every day—but seldom to eat soup. I use them to taste liquid-y dishes during cooking or to see if a warmed-up dish needs additional fresh seasoning. A metal spoon would burn my lips; the porcelain never does, and it somehow feels soft. When I'm tasting stock or soup, I ladle the liquid into the porcelain spoon through a small strainer, to remove the bits that are invariably floating in the liquid. Tasting with my "soft" porcelain spoon lets me focus on the nuances of taste rather than the discomfort of burning lips.

These are tools that make my kitchen life efficient and fun. Let me know[167] which tools *you* use—and love—the most.

---

[167] Please email me at drheidi@thecrazyeatingbook.com and we'll share your faves in our newsletter.